# MASTERING PRODUCT MANAGEMENT

A STEP-BY-STEP GUIDE

KEVIN BRENNAN

Mastering Product Management: A Step-by-Step Guide.

First edition (v1.3).



ISBN: 978-1-7338390-0-6

All feedback welcomed at:
feedback@mpmbook.com

# TABLE OF CONTENTS

# PREFACE

*Mastering Product Management: A Step-by-Step Guide* offers practical, real-world advice on the most important things a Product Manager will be involved with, and will deliver, in the quest for creating and capturing value. It covers the full new product cycle, from idea discovery through product end-of-life. Each section is short and concise, around two to three pages. Rather than dive deep into the theoretical background of a given area, the focus is on the critical steps a Product Manager would take to complete a given task.

Whether you're beginning your journey in product management or a seasoned practitioner, this book will help guide you through key activities and reorient you when necessary. The last section includes advice specifically for leaders of product teams and organizations. Although the focus of this book is on the management of technology products, the topics have broad relevance across industries.

Kevin Brennan
San Francisco, California

# DISCOVERY

# 1

# SETTING AN INNOVATION STRATEGY

*An innovation strategy is a master plan that guides the overall company, business unit, or product line innovation effort. Without the guidance and focus of an innovation strategy, business results usually suffer. Innovation efforts can be ad hoc, and often are operated independently of one another resulting in an incoherent collection of innovation projects. New product and service concepts emerge that seem attractive in isolation, but ultimately end up terminated as the company realizes that these ideas do not "fit" with the company's mission and competencies. Time and other resources are squandered. Overinvestment in the existing business is common as innovation efforts revert to the company's comfort zone. An innovation strategy brings focus and clarity to the innovation efforts, thereby increasing the probability that the company, business unit, or product line will successfully achieve its business goals. This section describes the key steps when creating an innovation strategy for a product line. These steps are also equally applicable to the company- or business-unit level.*

**Identify how innovation supports the product line strategy and goals.** Consider and define how innovation is connected to, and supports, the overall product line vision, mission, and strategy. What role does innovation play in meeting the product line business objectives?

**Define the level of innovation investment in existing and new areas.** Broadly speaking, the product line can invest in innovation related to its current business model and innovation related to new business models. For new business models, innovation can be "adjacent," involving expansion into new-to-the-product-line businesses or "disruptive," creating new-to-the-world markets and products. These are often referred to as Horizon 1 (existing), Horizon 2 (adjacent), and Horizon 3 (disruptive) innovations. The innovation strategy should define the relative investment in each horizon. For example, the strategy may dictate that "The product line will invest 60% of the innovation budget in Horizon 1, 25% in Horizon 2, and 15% in Horizon 3 innovation."

### Create innovation goals and objectives.

Goals provide a sense of purpose and direction and are broad in nature. Therefore, goals do not have to be specific enough to act on. Notably, innovation goals support the overall business unit or product line goals. Innovation objectives, on the other hand, are specific, precise, and easily validated. Objectives guide decision-making. For example, clear objectives help answer questions like the following: "Does focusing on this product, feature, customer, or partner help us achieve our innovation objectives?" Goals and objectives should be set for the existing business (Horizon 1) and new business (Horizons 2 and 3).

### Establish innovation guidelines.

Guidelines provide direction for the teams working on innovation and define the types of innovation sought. Innovation guidelines serve as an initial filter to reduce the number of innovation proposals. Innovation guidelines can also serve as a guardrail to avoid exceeding a specific level of risk.

### Identify "Strategic Arenas" to focus the innovation effort.

For each horizon, the innovation strategy should define the "strategic arenas" of focus: technologies, product areas, markets, etc. that the product line will and (as important) won't focus on. The strategic arenas will likely vary across each horizon of innovation. For each strategic arena, the innovation strategy should define how the product line will seek to participate in that area, for example, by being the first mover, a fast follower, the low-cost leader, a differentiator, or a niche player and how the product line will enter that arena, for example, internal product development, licensing, partnering, or acquisition.

### Set an innovation budget.

The innovation strategy becomes real when resources are allocated to the different areas of focus; for example, each of the three horizons and strategic arenas.

# 2

# SOURCING OPPORTUNITIES

*New ideas are essential to the future of all businesses, and the Product Manager plays a key role in sourcing and championing new ideas for the product or product line. The Product Manager for an existing product should always be on the lookout for ideas for new features and benefits that can add incremental value and sustain and grow the existing revenue. At other times, the company requires new-to-the-company products to meet its strategic growth objectives.*

## Define the goals of the search project and create constraints to guide the effort.

Define the motivation and goal for the high-level opportunity sourcing project. For example, is it to seek out new features for an existing product, consider expansion into a new market for the company with new products, or explore new-to-the-world ideas? Review the innovation strategy for the company or product line, if one exists, to ensure the search project aligns with the innovation strategy. Create guidelines and constraints to guide the opportunity sourcing effort. These "boundary conditions" will help guide the effort and increase the probability that the opportunity sourcing project will be successful.

## Choose the best opportunity sourcing technique(s).

Ideas and opportunities can come from many places including from the company's employees or entities outside the company. Depending on the goal and constraints for the search project, consider the best approach to searching for new ideas. Common idea sourcing techniques include the following:

- Using strategic analysis to source idea:
  - **Industry analysis:** Identify key changes and trends in the industry as a source of opportunity.
  - **Competitive analysis:** Analyze competitors' products, as well as your strengths and weaknesses, to prompt ideas.
  - **Market research:** Conduct primary or secondary research to understand a specific question related to target customers.
  - **Disruptive technologies:** Identify emerging disruptive technologies and ideate on a response.
  - **Core competencies analysis:** Assess the company's core competencies, strengths, and weaknesses to identify potential ideas that can take advantage of the company's unique strengths.
  - **Future scenarios analysis:** Create alternative scenarios of the future, including best and worst case, to prompt ideas.
  - **Patent mapping:** Analyze and synthesize information on patents related to an area of interest.
- Sourcing ideas from the company employees:
  - **Internal idea capture:** Solicit new product ideas from the company's employees, usually through a website or dedicated software.
  - **Ideation offsites:** Conduct periodic offsite meetings to scope out several major new ideas related to key areas for the product line.
  - **Innovation show:** Take advantage of company innovation shows to source ideas.
  - **Fundamental research:** Investigate new technologies through a corporate research and development (R&D) department.
- Sourcing ideas from customers:
  - **Customer interviews:** Organize cross-functional team visits to customers and conduct in-depth interviews to uncover ideas.
  - **Customer advisory board:** Elicit advice from a customer panel on how to solve for the search project.
  - **Customer focus groups:** Gather customers who are representative of the target market to discuss their needs and wants.
  - **Ethnographic research:** Observe customers as they use or misuse a product and look for insight into problem areas.
- Open Innovation:
  - **Partners and vendors:** Leverage expertise from partners and vendors.

- **Small businesses and startups:** Partner with young startups and small businesses in areas related to the search project (for example, forming strategic alliances, giving money to VCs to invest, or investing directly).
- **Universities:** Partner with universities to source ideas (for example, by funding research or employing professors and research students to do summer work alongside employees).
- **External submission of ideas:** Enable customers, users, and others outside the company to submit ideas, often over the internet. Another example is to run external idea competitions.
- **Crowdsourcing:** Invite the public to submit designs for finished products, not just ideas.

## Capture all ideas.

If an idea capture and management system does not exist, set one up to capture all ideas for the search project. An idea capture and management system is a key resource to assist with ongoing product management. Having one repository of all ideas allows the team to capture new ideas, even when there are no active idea search projects underway. That way, the team has an established repository of ideas available as a starting point for the next idea search project. The system should also capture prior ideas not pursued, and notes on that analysis for potential future consideration as technology or other market conditions change, thereby making past "parked" ideas relevant once again.

## Evaluate and select the best idea(s).

Compare all ideas resulting from the search effort to the constraints defined at the beginning of the project and identify which best meet the goals of the opportunity sourcing activity.

# 3

# INDUSTRY AND MARKET ANALYSIS

*The ability to monitor the wider industry or a market segment within an industry, recognize changes and trends, and apply that insight to the product strategy is critical to successful product management. It takes time to build up an understanding and perspective of the industry and to gain the judgment necessary to apply industry conditions and changes to the management of the product. Therefore, it is best to treat industry analysis as an ongoing activity and to set up a process for gathering data and conducting the analysis.*

## State the goals of the analysis.

Identify product management activities that will require and benefit from industry or market analysis. These can include new product discovery, new product planning, forecasting, and the annual strategic planning process. Identify how the analysis will facilitate these activities and then define an overall set of goals for ongoing analysis. Industry or market analysis can cover a wide array of topics and passively consuming data is of limited value. However, having clear goals and a keen sense of how the analysis will be used will bring focus to the effort and significantly increase the probability that the analysis will be effective. Define relatively static goals for the general, ongoing analysis. If there is a specific reason for updating the analysis, for example, to assist in the definition of a new version of a product, update the analysis with that specific goal in mind. Having an established process and current version of the analysis will make subsequent updates much easier and quicker.

## Define the areas to analyze.

Given the goals for the analysis, define areas to research and data to gather. For example:

- The size of the overall industry and specific market segments
- Industry and market segment growth rate
- Industry and market segment profitability
- Market attractiveness and opportunity
- Industry cost structure
- Macroeconomic indicators
- Changes in laws affecting the industry
- Changes in consumer attitudes

## Identify good sources of data.

Data can come from a multitude of sources. Identify the best given the goals of the analysis and the specific industry and market. Common sources of information include:

- Customer feedback
- The Sales team and channel partners
- Magazines and newspapers
- Trade journals
- Analyst reports
- Internet searches and Google Alerts
- Blogs
- Governmental agencies
- Professional associations
- Standards groups
- University research
- Primary market research

## Conduct the analysis.

Gather the necessary data and conduct the analysis. The areas to analyze will depend on the specific goals, but two popular frameworks that cover common areas of industry and market analysis are "PESTEL" analysis and "Porter's Five Forces" analysis. PESTEL covers many macro-environmental factors and is useful for understanding overall industry trends.

- **Political:** How the government impacts the industry including areas such as tax policy, tariffs, and government stability.

- **Economic:** High-level economic factors affecting the industry including interest rates, inflation rates, unemployment rates, and consumer confidence.
- **Social:** Income distribution, number of children, population growth rates, etc.
- **Technological:** Factors such as innovation spending, technological changes, and automation.
- **Environmental**: Includes climate change and waste management.
- **Legal:** Laws affecting the industry such as intellectual property law, employment law, and data protection.

"Porter's Five Forces" is another useful framework that focuses on the competitive intensity of an industry or market.

- **Industry rivalry:** The number of competitors, the strength of competitors, and the overall level of competitor rivalry have a significant impact on the industry. Low competitive rivalry provides a position of strength for your company and product and vice versa.
- **The threat of new entrants:** How easy or difficult is it for new competitors to enter the market? New entrants will decrease the profitability for established competitors in an industry. Many factors affect the ability of a new firm to enter an industry including barriers to entry, economies of scale, and switching costs.
- **The threat of substitutes:** A substitute offers a different way to solve the same problem. Attractive substitutes can weaken your position and reduce profitability.
- **Buyer power:** Buyer power is high if customers have many alternatives, if buyer concentration is high, and if switching costs are low.
- **Supplier power:** Supplier power is high when there are few suppliers, when the supplied item is differentiated, and ultimately when conditions exist that allow a supplier to increase their prices easily.

## Describe how industry and market conditions and trends may affect the future.

For each key area of analysis, summarize the past and the present and describe how the area may evolve and how that future state would affect the product and any actions needed to respond to the trend. For example, the emergence of a new technology could fundamentally change how current customers purchase the product, and the product strategy may need to be updated to take advantage of this trend.

**Share the analysis.**

For ongoing and specific analysis, share the analysis report with key stakeholders including the product team. Ongoing and insightful analysis will establish the Product Manager as a market expert and build the necessary credibility to be able to affect change and drive the product strategy over time. Sharing the analysis will also help establish a baseline and common understanding of the industry and market. The Product Manager is likely to get useful feedback from other stakeholders that will help deepen their understanding of the industry and market and highlight any gaps in the analysis to address in the future.

**Update the analysis regularly.**

Define the right cadence for updating the analysis. Industry and market analyses should be conducted as an ongoing process, and the Product Manager will continually review periodicals and market research, attend industry events, and encounter relevant industry data that should be noted for inclusion in the next update. However, the Product Manager should also carve out dedicated time regularly, ideally quarterly, to revisit the analysis and document and share the report with stakeholders.

# 4

# COMPETITIVE ANALYSIS

*Having a keen sense of the competitive landscape is central to successful product management. Competitive analysis should be a regular activity but can also be triggered by a new competitive entrant, a key competitive move such as a new product introduction or pricing change, or at various stages in the new product process such as during product definition or preparing for launch. The competitive analysis should identify competitors and assess them across relevant criteria as needed based on the goal of the analysis.*

## State the purpose of the competitive analysis.

Define the purpose of the competitive analysis. For example, is the analysis to identify and analyze current competitive offerings during new product definition or is the analysis in response to a new competitor entering the market?

## Identify the competition.

Identify the competitors that will be analyzed. Consider direct and indirect competitors including existing competitors and potential future competitors. Normally, the analysis would focus on one to three top competitors. Create a short company profile for each competitor.

## Define the assessment criteria and conduct the analysis.

Based on the goal of the competitive analysis, identify the key items that will be assessed for each competitor and conduct the competitive analysis using those criteria. Common items are listed below although some of these may or may not be applicable given the specific purpose of the analysis:

- **Leadership profile:** A short biographical summary of key members of the competitor management team.
- **Corporate culture:** The beliefs and behaviors that characterize the competitor.
- **Market share:** Estimate the market share of the competitors and identify whether their market share is increasing, decreasing, or flat and why.
- **Features and benefits:** Identify the features and benefits of the competitor offering. Look beyond the immediate product features to things like warranty, delivery, customer support, etc.
- **Cost structure and pricing strategy:** Estimate the competitor's cost structure (fixed and variable) and pricing strategy. What are the advantages and disadvantages of the cost structure and pricing strategy and how could they be exploited?
- **Channel:** How does the competitor sell and deliver the product to the customer (direct, intermediaries, etc.)?
- **Positioning:** How does each competitor position their solution using the Marketing Mix (Product, Price, Place, and Promotion)? For example, as a cost leader, differentiated solution, or niche player.
- **Marketing:** What marketing channels are being used? What is the competitor's marketing budget? How effective is their marketing?
- **Innovation strategy:** The competitor's approach to innovation and their R&D budget.

Good sources of competitive information include:

- Competitor websites
- Competitor product literature
- Customers
- The Sales team and channel partners
- Supply chain partners
- Media, including trade press
- Tradeshows and industry events
- Analyst reports
- Primary market research

**Identify competitor strengths and weaknesses.**
List the overall strengths and weaknesses of each competitor. Look beyond the immediate product features and benefits to include all aspects of the competitive offering, including corporate strengths and weaknesses, channel, etc.

**Assess future competitive moves.**
Identify how each competitor is likely to behave in the future.

**Do a SWOT analysis.**
From the perspective of *your* product, given the competitive landscape, what are your Strengths and Weaknesses, what Opportunities exist for your product and what Threats do you face from the competition?

**Summarize the analysis and state any recommendations.**
State the conclusion from the competitive analysis and identify any recommendations or resulting actions.

# 5

# MARKET RESEARCH

*Market research is an information gathering exercise to understand target customers. Customer insight is critical throughout the product life cycle including assisting with decisions on which customer problems to solve, validating aspects of the business model hypothesis, making tradeoff decisions on product features, assessing customer preferences, testing pricing, measuring awareness of your product and competitor products, and many other aspects of product management.*

**Define the research goal.**

Consider the core question to answer, the decision to make, or the insight required from the market research and define the resulting goal of the research. For example, the goal of the research may be to determine the unaided awareness of the product brand in order to establish a baseline to measure the efficacy of an upcoming marketing campaign.

**Create a mock final report.**

Create a version of the final report with fictitious data and review it with the stakeholders to determine whether the research meets the research objective. Iterate on the report until there is alignment on what the final deliverable should look like.

**Choose the best research method.**

Based on the research objective, identify the best research method to arrive at the needed insight. Given the complexities of conducting effective research, it is best to work with an expert on the research technique selection and the research design, if possible.

- **Primary research** is original research conducted by your company, often using an external market research agency. **Secondary research** involves gathering data that already exists. Secondary data can come from many sources including dedicated market research firms, government data, internal data, universities, magazines, or websites. In general, primary market research is more expensive and time-consuming than secondary market research. As a result, look to see if secondary research already exists and if it's accessible before considering primary market research. Common primary market research methods could include the following:
    - Surveys
    - Questionnaires
    - Focus groups
    - Interviews
    - Observations
- The type of information gathered by both primary and secondary market research can be either **qualitative** or **quantitative**. It's common to get a qualitative sense of the research area first and then seek to quantify the findings.

## Develop the research design.

Based on the chosen research technique, develop the research design. This includes things such as identifying research targets and deciding how to incentivize them to participate, deciding which questions to ask and crafting the questions, and logistics related to the research. Research design is a specialized profession and working with an expert is best, if possible.

## Gather and analyze the data.

Run the research (survey, focus group, etc.) and gather and analyze the data. Data is typically captured in a spreadsheet, analyzed, and summarized in tables and charts.

## Communicate the findings.

Summarize and document the research. Leverage the "mock" report if one was created (see above). State the research goal, identify the research technique used, summarize the findings, and answer the core question that prompted the research. Provide recommendations based on the research results.

# PLANNING

# 6

# PRODUCT VISION

*The Product Vision defines the purpose of the product or the overarching reason for creating the product. The Product Vision defines the "why" of the product without detailing "how" the vision is made a reality. It gives meaning to the day-to-day work of the Product Manager and the product team, acts as a guiding light when dealing with the inevitable setbacks and difficulties of product work, and helps provide direction in key decision-making. Although the Product Vision is a direct expression of the Product Manager's passion for the product, it impacts the wider team, and so it is typically best if the process used to create the Product Vision includes all key stakeholders working on the product. The many different views of the product are amalgamated into one cohesive Product Vision that unites the product team in their mission to make the product, and the related customer benefits, a reality.*

### Assess the target customers.

As a team, consider the target customers for the product. Who are they? What needs or wants will the product fulfill?

### Identify the key product features and benefits.

What are the most important features and benefits of the product? How do they help the target customers?

### Define how the product is different.

How do customers currently meet this need or want? How will the proposed product be different and better?

### Review the company and business unit vision.

Review and discuss the vision statements for the company and business unit if those vision statements already exist. Consider how the product will support the company and business unit vision and business objectives.

### Create a vision statement.

Given the target customers, the key product features and benefits, the competitive differentiation of the product, and the company and business unit vision and business goals, craft a vision statement that succinctly captures the reason for building the product. To ensure commitment from all stakeholders, do this as a collaborative effort. A good vision statement should be:

- **Meaningful** – States the important or useful purpose of the product
- **Inspiring** – Inspires the team to commit to the product's "cause"
- **Challenging** – Challenges and stretches the product team
- **Concise** – Is short and succinct
- **Durable** – Describes the future state the product is trying to create into the far future
- **Jargon-free** – Uses straightforward language

After writing the vision statement, double check that the Product Vision aligns with—and supports—the corporate and business unit vision for the future.

### Continually communicate the Product Vision.

Once created, the Product Manager should use every available opportunity to communicate and reinforce the Product Vision. Recalling the Product Vision during product team meetings and other similar forums is often a great way to center the audience and bring focus to the discussion.

# 7

# PRODUCT STRATEGY

*Product strategy is about how an organization will sustain and grow the business. Strategy work in product management involves the following key elements: analyzing and synthesizing the current business environment and identifying key business opportunities or challenges, determining the best way of responding to the opportunities or challenges, and building a coordinated product plan to execute the strategy.*

## Analyze and synthesize the current reality.

Product strategy work begins with an analysis of the current business environment. Very often the need for a new or updated product strategy is precipitated by changes in the market, for example, the introduction of a new technology, an economic downturn, a regulatory change, or a significant competitive move. The goal of this stage is to analyze and distill all the complexity of the current business environment into a simpler and actionable model of reality by analyzing the industry and market, determining what is important and what is not, and identifying the key business challenge or opportunity that the product strategy will address. The following activities can assist with this:

- **Industry and market analysis** – Analyze the wider industry and market and look for changes and trends that represent key business challenges or opportunities. Conduct a "Porter's Five Forces" analysis to understand the current and likely future competitive intensity and attractiveness of the market.
- **Competitive analysis** – Identify current and future competitors and do a competitive analysis. Summarize the competitive situation with a SWOT analysis: Identify the Strengths and Weaknesses of your company and product team and the Opportunities and Threats that exist given the competitive landscape.

- **Company analysis** – Consider how the company and product team have evolved. What skillsets, capabilities, competencies, and resources were developed and strengthened or lost or weakened, and how do these relate to the opportunities and challenges facing the company?

### Identify the best approach to the challenge or opportunity.

With the current market climate analyzed and the key product opportunity or challenge described, identify potential ways the product could address the challenge or opportunity and select the best path forward from the various options considered. This is the essence of product strategy: identifying the best approach to addressing the identified opportunity or challenge. The optimal product strategy will leverage defensible advantages that already exist or could be built that are unique to your company or organization and can include areas such as branding, channel, protected intellectual property, unique know-how, economies of scale, network effects, and cost advantages. The chosen approach or strategy serves as a general guideline for the body of work that subsequently must happen to execute the strategy. By selecting one path forward, the strategy rules out all other responses and brings focus to the efforts of the product team. Although the product strategy may not explicitly reference these areas, a good strategy will provide clear guidance in response to the following questions:

- What unique and defensible capability, advantage, or resource will the product leverage to best respond to the business opportunity or challenge?
- Should the product focus on being a low-cost leader or instead look to offer unique differentiation at higher cost? If the strategy is to focus on cost leadership, how will that position be established and defended? If pursuing a differentiation strategy, how will the product be different and how will that differentiation be protected?
- Should the product be offered to a mass market or a niche market?
- At a high level, how should the product be priced?
- What channels should be used to sell and deliver the product to customers?
- How should the product be positioned, marketed, and advertised throughout the sales cycle?

### Build a coordinated plan to execute the product strategy.

Strategy is powerless without action. The final critical element necessary when creating the product strategy is to build a high-level plan to execute the chosen path forward. Each key functional group working on the product including Development, Test, Manufacturing, Operations, Marketing, Sales, Finance, and Legal should create a high-level action plan to guide the strategy implementation. The functional plans do not need to include all actions and details required over the product life cycle, but they must have enough detail to show how each functional group will support the overall product strategy. To maximize the impact of the product strategy and make best use of the organization's resources, the functional plans need to be coordinated and also build upon each other.

**Monitor and update the strategy as needed.**

A product strategy is effectively a hypothesis about the best way to respond to changing business realities. The business environment is analyzed, assumptions are made, and a best path forward is identified. As the product team executes the strategy, the Product Manager should monitor whether the underlying hypothesis is being validated or invalidated. If things are not progressing as expected, the Product Manager should use that new knowledge to revisit the strategy and update it accordingly.

# 8

# BUSINESS MODEL

*The business model is the rationale for how a product creates, delivers, and captures value. The business model articulates the value of the product or service being offered, identifies one or more target market segments, defines the value chain to deliver the offering to the target market, and creates a way for getting paid. The term "business model" is often mistakenly used to describe the "revenue model" for a given business idea, when in fact the revenue model is a subset of the overall business model and focuses on how the company will get paid (see "Revenue streams," later).*

*A useful visual tool to assist with developing and documenting a business model is the Business Model Canvas created by Alexander Osterwalder. The Business Model Canvas is one of the key elements of Lean Innovation and serves several purposes:*

1. *It enables the team working on the new idea to see how the different elements of the business model fit together and support each other, and prevents obsessing over certain aspects of the business model at the expense of ignoring others.*
2. *It allows the business model hypothesis to be documented and easily revised as new facts and evidence are gathered from the market.*
3. *It facilitates discussion of the business model by the product team and with stakeholders outside the team.*

*In many companies, especially startups, the Business Model Canvas is replacing the more traditional Business Case, or the Business Case is created after the business model is validated. Drawing from the Business Model Canvas, the following are the key elements of any given product business model.*

**Value proposition.**
The key product features and benefits and how they solve customer problems; the quantitative value (for instance, price and speed of service) and qualitative value (such as design and customer experience) delivered to the customer.

**Customer segments.**
Who the product creates value for and the type of segment (mass market, niche, etc.).

**Channels.**
How the target customers want to be reached (direct or indirect channels) at different phases of the customer life cycle (awareness, evaluation, purchase, delivery, and after-sales).

**Customer relationships.**
How the business will keep and grow customers (for example, direct sales representatives, self-service, and communities).

**Revenue streams.**
How the company makes money with the product (product sale, licensing, leasing, subscription fee, etc.) and the pricing model for the product (fixed or dynamic pricing).

**Key activities.**
The things the company must do to make the business model work (for example, production, supply chain work, design services, etc.).

**Key resources.**
The most important assets to make the business model successful (for example, key intellectual property, buildings and laboratories, human resources such as engineers and scientists, and financial assets).

**Key partnerships.**
The suppliers and partners that make the business model work.

**Cost structures.**
The primary fixed and variable costs incurred in the business model.

# 9

# BUSINESS CASE

*A Business Case is used to evaluate and communicate the opportunity presented by the new product concept. The Business Case identifies the "customer problem" that the proposed product solves, analyzes the particular target market and assesses its attractiveness, and offers a financial analysis of the opportunity. The Business Case enables the management team to access the new opportunity on its own merits as well as compare the opportunity to other potential investment opportunities. The Business Case is also an important tool to assist with educating other stakeholders and gaining support for the new product. The Business Case evolves over time and is updated as necessary, often beginning with high-level analysis and becoming increasingly comprehensive over the product life cycle as insight is gained from customers and the wider market. Often, the Business Case includes the first expression of key product attributes such as the high-level features and the pricing model, and these are subsequently broken out and detailed in dedicated documents or tools. The Business Case is typically written as a document or a presentation.*

## Assess the high-level product opportunity.

- **Business need:** A description of the target customer and details of the need or want that creates the opportunity for the product.
- **Current solutions:** How the customer currently satisfies the need or want.
- **Product description:** A high-level summary of the proposed product including key features and benefits. Details of how the proposed product solves the customer problem in a new and valuable way.
- **Alternatives considered:** A summary of different ways of solving the market need that were considered and why the proposed solution was selected.

- **Timing:** The high-level schedule for the product project, key timing constraints, and the anticipated lifetime of the product.
- **Strategic fit:** How the proposed product fits with, and helps achieve, the company or business unit goals.
- **Organizational impact:** How the project will affect the organization including organizational structure and processes.

## Define and analyze the market for the product.

- **Market definition:** Characteristics, size, and growth of the target market. How the overall market is segmented and the target market segment or segments for the product.
- **Ecosystem:** A map and description of the ecosystem including suppliers, buyers, partners, and upstream and downstream ecosystem players. The value chain (who creates value for whom) and the flows of money in the ecosystem.
- **Trends:** Current patterns in the market that are creating the opportunity for the product as well as changes expected in the market over the lifetime of the product.
- **Competitive analysis:** A list of current and potential future alternatives; their features, benefits, and positioning; competitor strengths and weaknesses; and an assessment of the competitive advantage of the product.
- **Defensibility:** A statement about how to defend the proposed product against current and future competitors.
- **Barriers to entry:** An analysis of any key barriers to entry that exist in the target market such as competitor intellectual property, switching costs, economies of scale, and network effects.
- **Market attractiveness:** An assessment of the overall attractiveness of the market given supplier and buyer power, competitors, alternatives, the threat of new entrants, and other key attributes.

## Examine the financial aspects of the product opportunity.

- **Economic Value to the Customer (EVC):** The sum of all monetary and psychological benefits of the product relative to the closest substitute.
- **Pricing:** The intended pricing model for the product.

- **Profit and loss statement:** An analysis of the expected revenue, costs, and profit over the lifetime of the product including the net present value of the overall revenue stream, showing the expected return on investment for the product.
- **Scenario analysis:** An assessment of potential future scenarios of the profit and loss for the product based on different assumptions to show the "expected" outcome as well as possible alternative outcomes. Often "best case" and "worst case" scenarios are considered.
- **Cash flow projection:** Details of when money is spent and received.
- **Break-even analysis:** An estimate of when the product turns profitable, in unit volume and time.
- **Market cannibalization:** Details of how the proposed product will impact other products from the company.
- **Opportunity costs:** Alternative opportunities that are being given up to pursue the proposed product.

## Create a high-level plan and make a recommendation on the path forward.

- **Project plan:** A summary of the work needed to define, develop, launch, and manage the product for the full product life cycle including key milestones and estimates of resource needs from each functional group.
- **Recommendation:** A recommended course of action and guidance on the next steps.

# 10

# FINANCIAL ANALYSIS

*As the "Business Owner," the Product Manager must be intimately familiar with common financial tools, metrics, and nomenclature as they relate to the business segment and product. This section covers some of the most common and summarizes how they're calculated and used.*

## Units, price, and revenue.

Perhaps the most basic financial metric a Product Manager must be familiar with is the historical and anticipated revenue for the product. Calculate revenue by multiplying the unit volume by price. For example, 10,000 units sold for $2.50 each generates $25,000 in revenue. Price is often an average price across all units, or the average selling price (ASP). With two of these data points, the third can be calculated. Calculate ASP by dividing total revenue by total units, and total units are calculated by dividing total revenue by ASP. For example, if 1,000 units are sold for $2 per unit generating $2,000 in revenue, and 500 units are sold for $3 per unit generating $1,500 in revenue, the average selling price for the 1,500 units is $2,000 plus $1,500, or $3,500 total, divided by 1,500 units, or $2.33 per unit.

## Growth rate.

The growth rate for various key financial metrics is often a key consideration in product management decisions and discussions. Growth rate can be calculated for any period, with yearly and quarterly growth rate being the most common. Quarterly growth is often measured sequentially (quarter to quarter) and year over year. The growth rate is expressed as a percentage and is calculated using this formula:

*[(This Period – Last Period) / Last Period] x 100%*

For example, if revenue in year one was $1 million and revenue in year two was $1.5

million, then the year-over-year growth rate is $1.5 million less $1 million, or $0.5 million, divided by $1 million, or 50%.

## Return on investment (RoI).

The return on investment is the gain or loss generated on an investment relative to the amount invested. RoI is usually expressed as a percentage and used as a convenient way to measure the attractiveness of an investment or to compare investment options. RoI is calculated using this formula:

*[(Gains – Investment Costs) / Investment Costs] x 100%*

For example, if a company invested $10 million in a product that generated $50 million in revenue, the return on investment is $50 million less $10 million, or $40 million divided by $10 million, or 400%.

## Breakeven.

Breakeven is the point at which costs and income are equal, and therefore the initial investment is covered. Breakeven is expressed in the number of units and calculated using this formula:

*(Fixed Costs) / (Selling Price – Variable Costs)*

For example, if a product has fixed costs of $100,000, variable costs of $2 and a selling price of $4, breakeven occurs after 50,000 units.

## Payback period.

The payback period is the length of time required to recover the cost of an investment and is calculated by dividing the initial cash outlay by the amount of net cash inflow generated by the product per time period. Payback period is usually expressed as the number of years or quarters. For example, if the initial investment in a new product was $1 million and the product generates $200,000 quarterly, the payback period is $1 million divided by $200,000 or five quarters.

## "Profit and loss (P&L) statement" or "income statement."

A P&L statement shows the revenue and expenses for a product during a particular period. It's common to create a P&L statement at the beginning of a project to estimate revenue and expenses and justify the investment decision, and the P&L

is usually updated periodically during the product life cycle. The P&L statement is usually calculated for one or more years or quarters. At a high level, the P&L shows revenue, expenses, and profit. An example P&L statement is shown below for a three-year period.

| | Year 1 | Year 2 | Year 3 |
|---|---|---|---|
| Units | 100,000 | 200,000 | 250,000 |
| ASP | $3.00 | $2.50 | $2.25 |
| **Revenue** | $300,000 | $500,000 | $562,500 |
| | | | |
| Cost per unit | $1.00 | $0.80 | $0.75 |
| **Cost of Goods Sold** | $100,000 | $160,000 | $187,500 |
| | | | |
| **Gross profit** | $200,000 | $340,000 | $375,000 |
| | | | |
| Sales and Marketing | $100,000 | $100,000 | $50,000 |
| Research and Development | $150,000 | $50,000 | $10,000 |
| General and Administrative | $50,000 | $25,000 | $10,000 |
| **Operating expenses** | $300,000 | $175,000 | $70,000 |
| | | | |
| **Operating income** | –$100,000 | $165,000 | $305,000 |
| | | | |
| **Gross margin** | 67% | 68% | 67% |
| **Net margin** | –33% | 33% | 54% |

- **Revenue:** Units multiplied by the average selling price (ASP)
- **COGS (Cost of Goods Sold):** Units multiplied by the cost per unit
- **Gross profit:** Revenue minus COGS
- **Operating expenses:** Expenses not directly related to producing or manufacturing the product. These include:
  - Sales and Marketing
  - Research and Development
  - General and Administrative
- **Operating income:** Gross Profit – Operating Expenses

## Gross Margin and Net Margin.

Gross Margin and Net Margin are profitability ratios used to assess the financial health of a product and are calculated using data from the P&L statement. Gross Margin is the percentage of total revenue that the company retains after incurring the direct costs associated with producing the product. Net Margin is a measure of how much a company makes on the product after all expenses are covered. Both are represented as a percentage and calculated as follows:

*Gross Margin = (Gross Profit / Revenue) x 100%*

*Net Margin = (Operating Income / Revenue) x 100%*

# 11

# PRODUCT REQUIREMENTS

*Product requirements define what the product will do, and how it will work, in response to the market's needs. Requirements are often written in a document, spreadsheet, or dedicated software tool and typically evolve over time. Requirements serve as the basis for the broader effort of the product team in specifying, designing, building, and testing the product. Product requirements should identify the problem to be solved (the "what," articulated as requirements) without being prescriptive about how to solve the problem (the "how," defined elsewhere as product specifications).*

**Describe the customer using a persona and identify the customer's goals.** A persona is a brief description (less than one page) of a fictitious person used to represent the target market segment based on information and insight gathered from engaging actual target customers. A persona helps build empathy and makes the target customer less impersonal. Create personas for the end-user, the economic buyer, and other key people in the target market. Common elements of a persona include:

- Their name and a picture
- Their role, such as "end-user;" for B2B products, define the job title for the target persona
- Their profile:
    - Demographics: Age, gender, income, location, etc.
    - Psychographics: Personality, values, attitudes, interests, etc.
    - Behavioral attributes: Usage, brand loyalty, purchase occasion, etc.
- Their goals, the top things the persona is trying to accomplish
- Details of what is preventing the persona from achieving their goals with current solutions

## Define functional and non-functional product requirements to meet the customer's needs.

Once the customer or customers have been identified and described, and their needs and wants understood, craft functional and non-functional requirements for the product to meet those needs.

- **Functional requirements:** Functional requirements define what the customer would like to be able to do with the product to meet their needs; these requirements state what the product will do.
- **Non-functional requirements:** Non-functional requirements define how the product works. The following areas are common when defining how the product will work:
  - Performance (speed, capacity, durability, etc.)
  - Physical characteristics (size, weight, color, etc.)
  - Reliability
  - Supportability
  - Interoperability
  - Security
  - Regulatory
  - Internationalization
  - Channel
  - Demonstration
  - Documentation

## Define a high-level schedule for when different requirements are needed.

For each requirement or group of requirements, define the required release schedule and explain the rationale for the specified schedule.

# 12

# PRODUCT REQUIREMENTS IN AGILE

*Agile is a relatively new product methodology that began in software development and lends itself to products that are developed iteratively and incrementally. Scrum is the most widely used Agile framework. In Scrum, the "Product Owner" represents the interests of the business on the team and works to maximize the return on investment of the product. One key function of the Product Owner is to own and manage the Product Backlog, a list of all product requirements including new features, feature enhancements, bug fixes, documents, etc. This reference section summarizes key aspects of capturing and managing product requirements in Scrum.*

## User Stories.

The foundational element of the Product Backlog is the User Story. A User Story is a statement about something an end-user wants. User Stories define who the end-user is, what they want, and why they want it, often taking this form:

*As a <type of user>, I want <to do something> so that <reason or outcome>.*

At the beginning of a project, the Product Owner documents the key User Stories the product will address. Often, these are high-level representations of things the end-user wants to do. New User Stories will be added to the Product Backlog or modified in response to new information or market changes. When a User Story is being prepared for development, the team members will hold an in-person conversation about the story to establish a common understanding of exactly what needs to be done. The team will also identify the Acceptance Criteria, a series of pass/fail tests that are used to determine if the User Story was implemented as intended. The User Story, the team conversation and the resulting Acceptance Criteria combine to form a complete requirement specification for the product.

## Story Mapping.

The Product Backlog is a strict prioritization of User Stories, and often the number of User Stories can become large enough to the point where the relationship of User Stories to each other and the overall product starts to become unclear. Story Mapping is a technique that brings the focus back to overall product level by mapping out the different tasks a user completes in their use of the product. Headings list each step a user takes in their use of the product and User Stories are listed and prioritized in a grid under each key task. Different releases or versions of a product, including the "Minimum Viable Product," can then be defined by identifying which User Stories are to be included in each release.

## Managing the Product Backlog.

The Product Backlog is a dynamic, prioritized list of User Stories, describing all deliverables for the product. User Stories at the top of the Product Backlog are small chunks of work that are well-defined and will be implemented next. Often a User Story is initially a representation of a broad piece of work to be done and is placed lower in the Product Backlog. This is often called an "Epic." Before it is tackled, an Epic needs to be broken down into multiple, smaller, and better-defined User Stories with specific acceptance criteria. By concentrating on the User Stories that are close to being developed, those at the top of the Product Backlog, the team focuses its efforts on detailing only those features that are likely to be developed and avoids wasting detailed product definition effort on features that may not be developed.

# 13

# FEATURE PRIORITIZATION

*It is almost always the case that there will be more product features to develop than the product team has capacity for, and, therefore, a key decision facing the Product Manager and product team is which features to develop and when. This reference section discusses some approaches to feature prioritization.*

**Value versus cost.**

A simple way of prioritizing features is to create a graph of "value to customers" versus "cost to develop" and place each proposed feature on the graph. Features that place higher on value and lower on cost are ranked higher.

**Weighted scorecard.**

When the value to the customer or cost to develop are made up of different parts, it's useful to break those out and add a scoring component to the prioritization. Identify the constituent parts of cost and value, assign a weight to each, and calculate a weighted score to rank the features. An extension of this approach is to add other elements beyond cost and value to the prioritization criteria, and similarly assign a weight to those, score each feature, and arrive at a weighted score to create the prioritization. An example weighted scorecard is shown below for four features (A, B, C, and D) that are evaluated across four criteria: customer value, development cost, risk, and strategic alignment. Customer value and development cost are each broken into two example constituent parts.

| | | Score (out of 100) | | | |
|---|---|---|---|---|---|
| **Criteria** | **Weight** | **A** | **B** | **C** | **D** |
| **Customer Value** | **40%** | | | | |
| Time to market | 30% | 70 | 85 | 60 | 50 |
| Reduced costs | 10% | 35 | 65 | 30 | 80 |
| **Development Cost** | **30%** | | | | |
| Research and Development | 20% | 45 | 60 | 40 | 50 |
| Support | 10% | 65 | 85 | 35 | 40 |
| **Risk** | **15%** | 60 | 70 | 20 | 30 |
| **Strategic Alignment** | **15%** | 80 | 70 | 50 | 50 |
| **Weighted Score** | **100%** | **61** | **74** | **43** | **49** |

### The Kano Model.

The Kano Model is useful both as a feature prioritization tool, but also as a general philosophy to guide product definition. The Model holds that not all product features are created equal and that to be successful, the right amount of different classifications of features are required. Features are compared along two axes: (1) How satisfied the customer would be with a given feature, ranging from "frustrated" to "delighted" based on (2) the level of implementation of the feature, from "absent" to "fully implemented," as shown in the chart below. Question customers on potential features, and use the resulting data to place features in one of five categories:

1. **"Must Have"** features are expected by the customer. Although these features will not make a customer satisfied with the overall product, excluding these features will create customer dissatisfaction. Continuing to invest in Must Have features beyond the expected level of performance by the customer is pointless as it does not drive increased satisfaction.
2. **"Satisfiers"** are product features which have a satisfaction level that increases linearly with the given level of functionality. These are typically the core features that the product competes on in the market. Choose the right Satisfiers and the right level of implementation given the target competitive positioning.

3. **"Delighters"** are *unexpected* features that have a disproportionately high impact on customer satisfaction given the level of investment. A Product Manager should strive to have one to two Delighters in the product to create customer delight and positive competitive differentiation. Over time, as customers become more familiar with Delighters and as competitors imitate these features, the value of Delighters in customer satisfaction declines and they become Must Have features.
4. **"Indifferent"** are features that the customer doesn't care about. Eliminate these since they have no impact on customer satisfaction.
5. **"Reverse"** features are the opposite of Satisfiers in that the more that are added, the more dissatisfied the customer will be. It's important to monitor new features to ensure they are not, in fact, Reverse features, and if they are, to remove them.

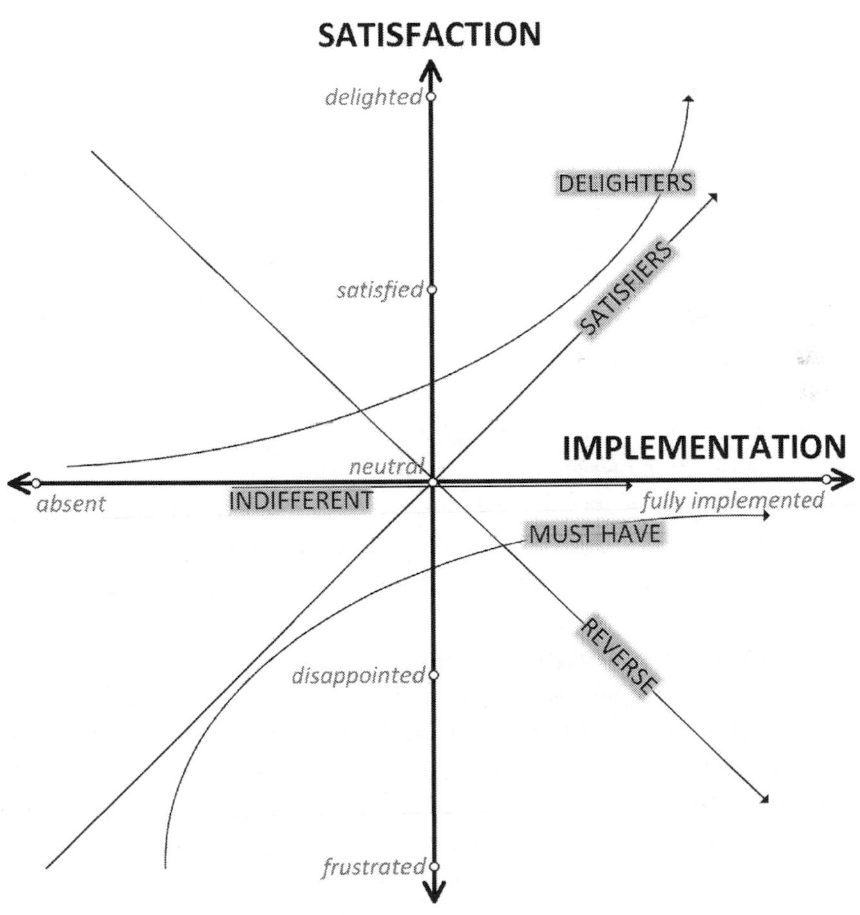

# 14

# ROADMAPS

*The overall scope of a product often needs to be broken out into a series of releases that occur over time. It is also common to release to market one or a few key features first, validate the market opportunity, and then follow-up with the full product scope. And as the market evolves, new product releases are typically required to meet new customer needs or in response to competitive moves. A Product Roadmap is a visual tool to show a series of product releases over time. The roadmap is very useful when facilitating alignment and when driving prioritization within the product team, when getting management buy-in for future investment in the program, and when ensuring broad alignment of different internal stakeholders including Sales and Marketing. Externally, a roadmap is used to show existing and prospective customers the plan for the product over time or in discussions with other external parties such as media and analysts. At the highest level, the Product Roadmap shows what will be delivered and when. Roadmaps can be created for a single product, a product family, a platform, an initiative, an underlying technology, or any other instance where related items occur over time. This reference section summarizes key considerations when creating both internal and external roadmaps.*

### Internal Product Roadmaps.

Create one or more versions of an internal roadmap with the level of detail dependent on the audience. A very detailed roadmap is required for alignment within the product team whereas a reduced set of information is typically better for other internal stakeholders. For each version or release of the product shown on the internal roadmap, the following items could be included:

- Release name and version number
- Internal codename
- Place in the new product process (for example, "Concept," "Planning," "Development," etc.)
- Statement on the business problem being solved
- Strategic alignment with key corporate or business unit initiatives
- A brief description
- Scope (key features)
- Milestones and schedule
- Dependencies
- Key target customers
- Percentage complete (if started but incomplete)
- Size (for example, "Small," "Medium," or "Large" based on predefined criteria)
- Priority (for example, "Low," "Medium" or "High")

## External Product Roadmaps.

The external roadmap is typically created using a subset of the information in the internal roadmap shown earlier. Some key guidelines for creating an external roadmap are listed below:

- Remove all sensitive data.
- Include a prominent disclaimer to note that the roadmap is not a commitment and is subject to change. It is critical that external parties are aware that while the roadmap is an expression of intent, it is not a committed plan.
- Use project code names to obfuscate the product or brand name in case the roadmap ends up in the hands of competitors.
- If you leave behind a version of the roadmap, consider creating two versions: The version that is presented and a "leave behind" version that further removes any sensitive data. Sometimes it's acceptable to present certain information verbally but leave that undocumented.
- If sending a roadmap to an external party, use a secure .PDF or another non-changeable format. If sharing the roadmap under a non-disclosure agreement, note that and include the name of the external partner on the roadmap.

# 15

# PRICING

*A product creates value by meeting a customer need or want. The role of Sales and Marketing is to communicate that value, and the role of pricing is to harvest the value. This section summarizes some of the key pricing-related activities in which a Product Manager is often engaged.*

## Estimating value.

Economic Value to the Customer (EVC) is the total *theoretical* price a customer should be willing to pay assuming they are fully informed about the benefits of the product and competing products. To estimate EVC:

- **Estimate the "Reference Value."** Identify the customer's best alternative to the product and the associated price.
- **Calculate the "Differentiation Value."** Estimate and sum the value of the benefits of the product and subtract all costs unique to the product, including switching costs.
- **Determine the EVC.** Economic Value to the Customer is the competitive Reference Value plus positive Differentiation Value less negative Differentiation Value. In general, the price for the product should be set between the Reference Value and the EVC (see "Pricing a new product," later).

## Measuring willingness to pay (WTP).

Estimating willingness to pay, or the most a customer is willing to pay for the product, is a fundamental step in setting the price, either for the overall product pricing scheme or an individual customer deal. Willingness to pay can be estimated using the following techniques:

- Analyzing historical sales data from past purchases of the product or similar products.
- Using direct questioning, interviews, and surveys to understand purchase intentions.
- Doing conjoint analysis, where customers trade-off price and features.
- Experimenting in a test market, by selling the product to a small number of target customers.
- Conducting in-store or laboratory experiments where customers are unaware they're participating in a pricing experiment.

## Pricing a new product.

Key steps in pricing a new product include the following:

- **Estimate the price ceiling.** The price ceiling is the total Economic Value to the Customer, EVC, discussed earlier. This is the most that can be charged for the product.
- **Determine the price floor.** The price floor is set by estimating the marginal cost of the product and then adding the desired profit margin. Although the actual price should not be set using this "cost-plus" calculation, the price will likely need to at least cover this price floor or else the business case for the product likely does not make economic sense.
- **Identify the launch position.** Identify how similar the new product is to existing solutions. New products are either revolutionary, evolutionary, or "me-too." The closer the product is to existing solutions, the lower the Differentiation Value, and the closer the price will need to be to the competitive Reference Value.
- **Measure willingness to pay.** WTP is the most a customer is willing to pay for the product, discussed earlier.
- **Assess likely competitive responses.** Evaluate how competitors are likely to respond to the new product pricing and the impact of that on the pricing strategy.
- **Consider the product category life cycle.** Product categories move through a life cycle with these broad stages: introduction, growth, maturity, and decline. Identify the stage the overall product category is in, and consider how that will affect the pricing strategy for the new product. For example, during the introduction phase of the life cycle, the value of the new product

category and individual products in that category are not well understood, and therefore the focus is on customer education. In general, customers in the introduction phase are price-insensitive, and often a skimming price strategy makes sense. In the maturity phase of the category life cycle, competition is usually intense, and customers are price-sensitive, and so a neutral pricing strategy is often used. Consider the stage of the category life cycle and how that will impact the product pricing strategy.

- **Define the pricing strategy.** Three high-level pricing strategies exist:
  - Skimming – Price high to capture more margin at the cost of a lower market share.
  - Penetration – Price low and sacrifice some margin with the goal of winning market share.
  - Neutral – Price competitively and seek to win market share in other ways such as through superior marketing.
- **Estimate cannibalization of existing products.** Consider the potential impact of the new product pricing on existing products and use that to inform the pricing.
- **Set the pricing model.** Many different pricing models exist (including per unit, per usage, subscription, sliding scale, two-part pricing, and freemium), the details of which are outside the scope of this book. Research and identify the optimal pricing model for the specific product considering the price ceiling and floor, willingness to pay, the launch position, the category life cycle, likely competitive responses, cannibalization effects, and the overall pricing strategy.
- **Set the pricing policy.** Set the internal policy for things such as discounts and bundling with other products.
- **Enable value and price communications:** Support the Sales and Marketing team with the necessary collateral and training to communicate the product value to customers and to justify the price.

## Reacting to competitive price reductions.

A good first step when considering a competitive price reduction is to calculate the percentage breakeven sales change given the new competitor price by dividing the price reduction by the product contribution margin. For example, if a competitor reduces the price by 10%, the percentage breakeven sales change for a product that was selling at $60 with a $30 contribution margin is $6 divided by $30, or 20%. As a first-order analysis, if you believe that by not matching the competitor price, sales volume will reduce by 20% or less, then it is better not to match the competitor price change. A more refined approach is to estimate the total cost of reacting to the competitive price reduction as well as the strength of the competitor and respond in one of four ways:

- **Ignore** – Ignoring the competitive move is prudent when the competitor is weak and when the cost of reacting outweighs the benefits. Matching the price reduction may also only precipitate a further, more painful reduction.
- **Accommodate** – When the competitor is strong, and the cost of matching a competitive price reduction is high, it is best to accommodate the competitive move.
- **Defend** – When a response is cost-justified, and the competing firm is strong, the firm should defend their pricing. The goal here is to convince the competitor to "play nice" and to signal that aggressive pricing is not in the competitor's best interest.
- **Attack** – Often a weak competitor misjudges their market strength and initiates a price reduction in the hope of gaining market share only to be outdone by a strong competitive response.

# 16

# FORECASTING

*Forecasting is the process of estimating the future demand and revenue for a product. Forecasting is used to assist with investment decisions in new products, to drive manufacturing, to set budgets, as part of the strategic planning process, and to guide Sales and Marketing efforts.*

## Gather and synthesize relevant data.

Gather and review existing data and define and conduct research efforts as needed to gather additional data to assist with the forecasting effort. Good sources of data for forecasting include:

- Historical sales data for the product or for similar products
- Forecasts from the Sales department
- Customer input
- Competitor data
- Distributor and channel partner data
- Primary and secondary market research
- Input from a panel of experts (the Delphi method)
- Industry and trade association reports
- Government data such as census data

## Estimate the total market size (TAM).

TAM, or Total Available Market, is an estimate of the size of the overall market for the product. Calculate TAM by multiplying the total number of units expected to sell in the market during the forecast period by an estimated average selling price (ASP) to arrive at a revenue estimate for the total market.

### Segment and estimate the size of the target segment (SAM), if applicable.

If the product is not a mass market product and is instead focused on a subset of the overall market, segment the market and similarly estimate the size of the target market segment. This is the Serviceable Available Market (SAM). SAM and TAM are identical if the product is targeting the whole market.

### Estimate the Share of Market (SOM).

Finally, estimate the part of the Serviceable Market the product will capture for the forecast period, the Share of Market (SOM). Usually, SOM is a fraction of SAM, which is, in turn, a fraction of TAM. The Total, Serviceable, and Share of Market are represented a few ways:

- TAM, SAM, and SOM can be represented in absolute terms as units and revenue.
- SAM is also often represented as a percentage of TAM.
- SOM is often represented as both a percentage of TAM and as a percentage of SAM, depending on the context.

### Compare the "top-down" forecast to a "bottom-up" forecast.

Some products lend themselves better to top-down forecasting where you begin with an overall population for TAM and drill down to SOM. Other products, especially products with a highly concentrated customer base, can be more accurately forecasted by estimating the demand on a per-customer basis. Ideally, both a top-down and bottom-up estimate should be created to cross-check the forecast for accuracy.

### Create worst-case, expected, and best-case estimates.

Define the expected forecast and then calculate a best-case and worst-case forecast to show how the forecast could vary depending on a stated set of assumptions. This is useful to show that the forecast is just an estimate and that the actual results could vary, for better or worse. A common mistake is to focus on the potential upside, the best-case, while ignoring the downside potential of the forecast.

### List and validate the forecast assumptions.

Identify and document all key assumptions and work to validate those assumptions. Review the assumptions with key stakeholders to seek feedback and update the forecast accordingly. Assumptions can include things like seasonality, expected competitive moves, and return rates.

### Publish the forecast.

Publish and share the forecast. The numerical part of the forecast should be captured in a spreadsheet as errors can be introduced by manually manipulating numbers in a document. It is useful to accompany the spreadsheet with a document to capture all key information including the sources of all data, key assumptions and a discussion of the assumptions, and a summary of the expected outcome as well as the best-case and worst-case forecasts. For forecasts where prior results are available, compare the prior forecast to actual results and explain any variances.

# 17

# RISK MANAGEMENT

*Risks are uncertain events or conditions that, if they occur, will harm a product's success. Risk planning is a key activity for product teams and is usually started during the planning phase and updated and monitored throughout the product life cycle. Risk planning involves foreseeing risks, estimating impacts, and defining plans to eliminate or minimize the risks.*

## Identify potential risks.

Identify all potential risks by working with representatives of all functional groups working on the product. Common risks categories include:

- Cost
- Schedule
- Scope
- People
- Technical
- Market
- Legal
- Strategy

## Evaluate and prioritize each risk.

Evaluate each risk based on an estimate of the probability the risk will occur (low to high) and the potential impact (low to high). Rank and prioritize the risks. Identify those risks that are important enough to warrant a mitigation plan.

## Write risk statements.

Write a risk statement for each key risk. The statement should identify what the potential event is and what the consequences are if the event comes to pass.

## Decide on the mitigation plan.

Mitigate risks in one of four ways:

1. Risk avoidance: Develop an alternative strategy. This often involves higher cost.
2. Risk sharing: Partner with others to share the risk, for example, a joint venture.
3. Risk reduction: Take steps to reduce the risk. For example, by hiring experts to work on a part of the product development with which the team is unfamiliar.
4. Risk transfer: Shift the risk to a different party. Insurance is a common example.

## Assign an owner to each risk.

Assign an owner to each key risk, ideally the person who has the most knowledge about the risk and the authority to execute the mitigation plan.

## Track and monitor risks.

Document the risk management plan and review the risks frequently at the product team meeting and in stakeholder review meetings to understand the current status, whether risks have changed, and if new risks have emerged. Communicate changes to key stakeholders including when risks are resolved.

# 18

# DECISION-MAKING

*Product Managers spend much of their time at the hub in a network of information flows with the product team, Sales and Marketing, customers, distributors, partners, and other stakeholders key to the success of their product and business. The Product Manager needs to be able to identify and interpret key information and signals from this network and decide how to respond to ever-changing realities such as customer feedback on features and benefits, competitor price changes, or revised schedule estimates from the development team. Often, the success or failure of a product depends on the Product Manager's ability to make good and timely decisions, both as an individual and as part of a team.*

## A generic decision-making framework.

The following steps can be used to guide the decision-making process for decisions that are to be made as an individual or as a team.

- Define the decision to be made.
- List all important constraints and criteria.
- Gather data and develop decision options.
- Decide by selecting the best option.
- Communicate and implement the decision.

## Group decision-making.

A Product Manager will often work with a team, usually the product team, to make decisions. When managing decisions as a team, it is useful to establish a framework for making decisions with defined roles and responsibilities. One common approach is the DACI model, with the following roles and responsibilities:

- **Driver** – The Driver is the person who facilitates the decision-making process and ensures that a decision is made. The Driver works to make sure that the decision is properly formulated, that the right people are involved, that decision options are created, and that the decision is documented and communicated.
- **Approver** – The Approver is the one person who makes the decision.
- **Contributors** – Contributors are subject matter experts on important areas related to the decision. The Driver works with Contributors to formulate decision options. Sometimes the Driver and Contributors will offer a recommendation on the best option for consideration by the Approver.
- **Informed** – These are stakeholders that are informed of the final decision.

## Key decision-making considerations.

When faced with a decision, consider the importance of the decision, whether the decision can be reversed or not after the fact, and the relative priority of deciding fast versus taking more time to improve the confidence level in the decision.

- **Importance:** It's often useful to initially classify the decision in terms of its potential impact (low to high), both positive and negative. The categorization will help guide the appropriate effort to invest in the decision, including estimating how much time to spend on the decision, how many people to involve, and how much information is needed to make the decision. In general, the less important a decision, the less time and effort should be spent on it. The essence of "good" decision-making is to invest the appropriate amount of time and resources given the importance of the decision.
- **Reversibility:** For significant or "high impact" decisions, a key consideration is whether the decision can be reversed or not once made. Most decisions can be reversed. However, critical decisions that cannot be reversed should be approached carefully and demand a greater degree of analysis and consideration.
- **Speed:** Often, it is more important to decide, commit to a path forward, and get going than to spend time overly detailing and refining alternative options. Although a "better" path forward could exist, the effort or time required to uncover it may not be justified. Consider the benefit of making a quick yet satisfactory decision and moving forward relative to the benefit of spending more time deciding. In general, consider the appropriate timeframe for the decision, set a deadline, and list that as a key constraint in the decision-making process.

# 19

# STAKEHOLDER MANAGEMENT

*Relative to a new product, a stakeholder is any individual or group that can affect or be affected by the product. Most projects have a variety of stakeholders, often with different and competing interests and therefore stakeholder management is an important part of successfully delivering a new product. This section describes key steps in stakeholder management by the Product Manager in a new product project.*

## Identify all stakeholders, internal and external.

Stakeholders can be internal to the company or external. Start by creating a list of all potential stakeholders. For the Product Manager, this often includes:

- The leaders on the product team including the Engineering Lead, UX Lead, the project manager, and their managers.
- Your manager and your manager's manager.
- Everyone that has input to, and approval of, funding decisions and other project reviews and exits.
- Team leaders and partners in key Marketing functions including Marketing Communications, Market Research, and Branding.
- Your Finance, HR, and Legal partners.
- Customers, key account managers, and the leaders of the Sales organization.
- External partners, including vendors and distributors.
- Media and key influencers.

### Assess stakeholder interest and power.

Analyze each stakeholder in terms of the power they have to advance or block the new product project and their level of interest in the product.

- **High Power, High Interest (Manage Closely):** These stakeholders have the biggest impact on the product and therefore need to be managed closely. Stakeholders in this category include very important customers and budget holders and approvers of key resources on the product project.
- **High Power, Less Interest (Keep Satisfied):** These stakeholders have significant power and need to be kept satisfied, yet they have a lower interest in the product and therefore need less interaction. These could include the VP of Engineering; while part of her organization is involved in the product team, the product is often only one of many products with which her organization is involved. The VP has the power to negatively affect resourcing, for example, but has lower direct interest in the product.
- **Low Power, High Interest (Keep Informed):** The product can materially affect these stakeholders, but they don't have the power to make decisions. Often, these are individual contributors that are heavily involved in the work of the new product project. It's important to engage these stakeholders as they can be allies in building support for key decisions.
- **Low Power, Less Interest (Monitor):** These stakeholders should be monitored, and the level of communication should be kept to a minimum.

### Create and implement a stakeholder management and communication plan.

Now that the key stakeholders are identified, analyzed, and prioritized, create a stakeholder management plan that spans the product life cycle to engage and communicate with stakeholders to ensure their needs and objectives are being met, to build support for your objectives and for key product decisions, and to address any issues as they arise. Key aspects of the plan include:

- Identifying the objectives, interests, and agenda of each key stakeholder as it relates to the product. This requires meeting the key stakeholders in-person, and it often takes time to build an accurate understanding of stakeholder objectives.

- Detecting where your interests are aligned with key stakeholders and where there are potential conflicts and planning to address those conflicts.
- Detailing what you want from each stakeholder or group of stakeholders and how you will accomplish those goals.
- Communicating with key stakeholders and groups of stakeholders. Some stakeholders will require light communications, maybe through a periodic status report, whereas other stakeholders will require much more communication including in-person meetings and product demos, for example. Identify what needs to be communicated, when, and how.

# DEVELOPMENT

# 20

# LEAN INNOVATION

*Most innovations fail, not from a deficit of technology or failure in product development, but from a lack of paying customers. To avoid the "lack of customers" trap, Lean Innovation Management ("Lean") focuses first on testing the appetite for a new product concept with customers and validating the new business model before significant resources are dedicated to the expensive tasks of fully developing, launching, selling, and marketing the product. The Lean approach is optimal for products with new-to-the-company business models, "horizon 2 and 3 innovations" in Lean nomenclature, where most—if not all—aspects of the business model are new and unknown.*

*Lean uses the scientific method of experimentation to validate the hypotheses that the product's business model is built upon by conducting hundreds of in-market experiments with customers, users, buyers, partners, and other ecosystem players to arrive at an evidence-based perspective on the attractiveness of the proposed new product. It does this with speed and urgency, thereby reducing risk and minimizing cost and time.*

*Lean can be described in two phases. In the first phase, Customer Discovery, product-market fit is tested. Opportunities that emerge with product-market fit validated are then applied to a second phase, Customer Validation, where the scalability and repeatability of the potential new business are tested. The key steps in Lean Innovation from the perspective of a Product Manager are summarized below, drawing from the work of Steve Blank, Eric Ries, and Alex Osterwalder.*

**Lean phase 1: Customer Discovery.**

In the beginning, the new product concept is really a collection of guesses, estimates, and assumptions about various parts of the business model: who the customers are and how to reach them, the problem being solved, what needs to be done to solve the customer problem and assets needed to do that work, what partnerships are needed, and how to make money.

- **Create the Business Model Canvas:** Start by deconstructing the business model for the new product concept into its constituent parts and graphically represent them on a one-page Business Model Canvas.
- **Size the market:** Do an initial estimate of the size of the overall market, the target market segment, and the anticipated share of market to get an early read on whether the new product concept offers an attractive enough opportunity to warrant further analysis and investigation.
- **Identify experiments:** Write short one-page briefs for each of the nine elements of the business model and identify tests or experiments that will be used to prove or disprove the key aspects of the hypothesis for each part of the business model.
- **Get out of the building:** Engage potential customers and other parts of the target market to run the identified experiments and gather feedback. Hypotheses are either validated, invalidated, or modified. Iterations are small refinements to the business model whereas pivots are a substantial change, such as modifying the pricing model or target customer segment. Update the Business Model Canvas with each change. Iterations and pivots are again validated or invalidated through experimentation, and the cycle continues.
    - Examine the "problem" first: The first area explored is how important the "problem" is to the market: in other words, the potential for the new business. This phase seeks to answer the following questions: Do we really understand the customer's problem, and do enough people really care about the problem for this to become a viable business? The focus is initially on the problem and not the solution.
    - Then test the value prop: Next, the value proposition for the product concept is tested with customers to see whether they're excited enough to eventually buy and use the proposed new product. A low-fidelity minimum viable product (MVP) is used to test different aspects of the business model. Unlike the traditional "waterfall" development methodology where a product is developed serially (requirements, specifications,

alpha, beta, first customer ship, GA, etc.), Lean, leveraging Agile development, introduces the proposed product incrementally to customers, enabling continuous customer feedback through development.

- Confirm initial product-market fit: The other aspects of the business model hypothesis are then tested including pricing, channel, and the target market segments. In the end, the Business Model Canvas is updated based on all insight gathered and the product team decides whether they have achieved product-market fit: Has a significant enough problem been identified which many people want to be solved and does the proposed product solve the problem in a compelling way?

## Lean phase 2: Customer Validation.

After validating initial product-market fit, the team then proceeds to the second phase where the scalability and repeatability of the business model are tested. In the Customer Discovery phase, a low-fidelity minimum viable product (MVP) was used to gauge interest in the new venture, but the team did not try to actually sell the proposed product. In the Customer Validation phase, the team now tries to sell the product and acquire customers or users.

- **Test scalability and repeatability:** A high-fidelity MVP with the core product features is created along with data sheets and other collateral to assist the sales process. Simultaneously, product positioning and messaging are developed and tested. Ultimately, the team is looking to determine whether the business can scale (customer revenue exceeds acquisition costs) and is repeatable (knowing the right prospects to acquire).
- **Pivot and repeat if necessary:** It's common that the team will conclude at this stage that the business model is not scalable because some part of the business model hypothesis was invalid (for example, a misunderstanding of the correct channel to use). At that point, the team typically pivots and makes a material change and goes through the process again to revalidate the new business model. It often takes several passes before a market is truly understood.
- **Refactor before scaling:** Once the business model is validated and proven to be scalable and repeatable, the product is now ready to go through a refactoring stage to eliminate technical and organization debt accrued in the fast-paced Customer Discovery and Customer Validation processes before the business is actually scaled.

# 21

# MAKING TRADEOFFS

*Changes are often required to the product plan during development based on market changes such as an update to the schedule of a lead customer, competitive announcements, changes in resources in the development team, or any other change that has an impact on the new product project. The Product Manager plays a key role in guiding and assisting the product team with making tradeoff decisions when a change is needed, as summarized in the steps below.*

### Build a baseline plan.

At the end of the "planning" phase, a baseline plan is generated by the product team that captures all key work items, their duration, start and completion dates, and dependencies. A good baseline plan is critical to being able to make informed tradeoffs.

### Define the requested change.

Any number of events can trigger requests for changes. A customer may require a change to a feature, budgets could be modified during the annual budgeting process, or Engineering may determine that a given work area requires more time based on preliminary work. Define the requested change such that the Project Manager and the product team can understand and evaluate the ask.

### Create tradeoff options.

Based on the change request, the product team should evaluate different ways to accommodate the change by varying some other aspect of the plan. The "Project Triangle" is a popular model for assessing tradeoffs and focuses on the potential tradeoff between scope, schedule, and cost. However, there are likely other variables that can be changed to accommodate a given request. Here are key variables to consider:

- Scope
- Schedule
- Cost
- Quality
- Risk
- Resources
- Market impact
- Strategic impact

Sometimes it's not possible to make a tradeoff in one area. For example, there may be times when adding more capacity to the Engineering team will have no immediate impact such as when the existing team is already fully occupied and therefore doesn't have time to absorb the extra capacity. When evaluating tradeoffs, confirm that the tradeoff is actually possible given the realities of the project.

**Evaluate the tradeoffs and decide.**

Meet as a team to discuss and evaluate the tradeoffs and make the tradeoff decision. See the Decision-Making section for an overview of an approach to making decisions as a team.

# 22

# PRODUCT TEAM MEETINGS

*The product team is a cross-functional team chartered with managing the product, ideally through the full product life cycle, from concept through end-of-life. The product team is like the board of directors or the "C-Suite" for the product. Representatives from each key functional group (Product Management, Engineering, Design, Program Management, Finance, etc.) are assigned to the team, and they have the authority to make decisions on behalf of their department. Best practices for running successful product team meetings are summarized below.*

## Define team membership, roles, and responsibilities.

Product teams usually have at least two levels of membership. The "core team" are full-time members of the team and are responsible for the ongoing leadership of the product. The "extended team" is comprised of representatives from functional groups that are periodically called upon to assist or advise the core team or to participate fulltime on the product team at a specific part of the new product process, for example, to assist with the product launch. The product team should have a documented definition of each role on the team and the key responsibilities of that role. For example, the Product Manager typically plays the role of "Business Owner" and sets the product vision and strategy, owns the Product Roadmap, and prioritizes features. Defining roles and responsibilities will help ensure alignment across the team members regarding who does what, reducing potential friction.

## Clarify decision-making authority.

Discuss how the team in general will make decisions, and specifically consider the process for making key decisions that the team is likely to encounter including decisions related to features, budget, release acceptance, etc. See the Decision-Making section for an approach to group decision-making.

### Assign a meeting organizer.

Identify who on the team will organize the team meetings and identify a protocol for when team meetings can be canceled. Often, the Program or Project Manager is responsible for organizing team meetings, and that person also has the responsibility for canceling or moving meetings if needed.

### Decide on meeting frequency.

Decide how often the team will meet. Ideally, the team should meet once a week, especially from the concept phase through product launch. Once decided, keep the team meeting at the same time and for the same duration. Infrequent meetings or meeting at different times breaks the momentum and discipline of the team.

### Establish rules on attendance.

Define who needs to attend each team meeting and who may optionally attend. Typically, core team members attend each meeting, and the core team decides when to invite extended team members. Decide on the quorum, the minimum number of team members that need to be present for a meeting to proceed and for making decisions. Establish rules for substitute attendance and the decision authority of substitutes.

### Manage the agenda.

Good agenda management is critical to running successful meetings. Identify who on the team will own the creation and management of the agenda for each meeting. The agenda manager should seek input on the agenda for the next team meeting ahead of time, finalize the agenda, and send it ahead of time to team members. Team members should review the agenda and come prepared to address each topic. Establish a protocol for canceling meetings if there is no agenda or if the agenda is insufficient to warrant a meeting. Common agenda items include:

- Confirm quorum
- Review the meeting agenda, consider any changes, and finalize it
- Review the meeting minutes of the last meeting
- Status update from each functional group

- Market and customer updates
- Financial updates
- Issues
- Risks
- Action items

**Create and distribute meeting minutes.**

At the beginning of each meeting, identify who will take meeting minutes. Distribute meeting minutes within 24 hours of the meeting. Common meeting minutes items include:

- Meeting date
- Attendees and absentees
- Summary of topics covered
- Decisions made
- Action items

# 23

# DAILY STANDUP MEETINGS

*In Agile software development, a Daily Standup meeting is held each workday during a sprint. The meeting is short, 5 to 15 minutes, and is used by the development team as a way to communicate what was done since the last standup, what they will do today, and to surface any obstacles impeding progress. Best practices for Daily Standups are noted below along with guidance for product staff attending the meeting.*

## Best practices for Daily Standup meetings.

- Keep it short, 5 to 15 minutes.
- Meet at the same time, duration, and location each day, ideally at the beginning of the day.
- Meet where the work happens.
- All development team members should attend and participate.
- The Scrum Master organizes the Standup meeting but the role of Facilitator should be rotated through each team member to avoid turning the meeting into a status reporting session to the Scrum Master.

## Product Owner, Product Manager, and the Daily Standup.

In Agile, the Product Owner is responsible for defining user stories, managing the backlog, and accepting user stories as done. Sometimes the Product Manager is also the Product Owner. There is some debate within the Agile community on whether the Product Owner or the Product Manager should attend the Daily Standup. (My perspective is that the Product Manager and Product Owner should periodically attend the Daily Standup but as a passive participant.) The Standup is intended primarily for the team doing the work to build and test the product. However, the Product Manager and Product Owner can benefit from attending by getting up to date on the sprint status and understanding any obstacles. Here are some key considerations from the perspective of the product staff and the Daily Standup:

- Be an active listener but not an active participant. Use the meeting to get a sense of progress and obstacles as well as the capacity and velocity of the team.
- Do not attend daily but do attend frequently, perhaps once or twice a week, and attend on the same days each week if possible for continuity.
- Be sure the team is not reporting status to you. Ask them to report status to each other.
- Answer any quick questions for the team if asked, for example, to clarify a requirement, but avoid getting into details.
- Avoid taking on Scrum Master duties related to the Daily Standup.

# 24

# BETA TESTING

*Alpha testing is testing of the incomplete product, usually a subset of features, by internal testers during product development. Beta testing is testing of an early version of the final product by a targeted number of real users external to the company to determine if the product works as expected and to uncover any bugs or issues to fix before making the product generally available. Beta testing is a critical precursor to product launch and serves to give the Product Manager confidence that the product functions correctly and that the quality level is sufficient before releasing the product to the wider market.*

## Define goals and metrics.

Create specific and measurable goals for the beta testing. Is the goal to test all features, specific features, the out-of-box experience, support documentation, or some other goal? Define only a small number of realistic goals to cover the most important things to test. Create metrics to measure the goals.

## Identify target testers.

Given the beta testing goals and the type of product, create a profile of the ideal target tester and identify the number of testers required for the beta program. Focus on testers that are representative of the target customers for the product. Consider how to source testers and any incentive scheme necessary to motivate participation.

## Create milestones and a schedule.

Identify key milestones and draft a schedule for the beta program. Key milestones include when the product will be ready for testing, when tester acquisition occurs, when testing will be complete, and when results will be gathered and analyzed.

### Set the budget.

Estimate the budget needed to run the beta program including sourcing and incentivizing participants, equipment, and the results-gathering effort. Secure approval for the budget.

### Recruit testers and run the testing.

Recruit target testers and educate them on the program goals and duration. Describe how the testers will report results and how they will be compensated, if applicable. Have testers sign a beta participant agreement and a non-disclosure agreement (NDA).

### Gather and analyze the results.

Collect, analyze, and discuss the outcome of the beta testing with the product team and identify how to address the results. In particular, plan to deal with any bugs or issues that beta testing uncovered.

# LAUNCH AND MARKETING

# 25

# MARKET SEGMENTATION

*Segmentation is the process of dividing the overall target market into sub-groups based on some common characteristic to identify and target the most attractive segments. A product that tries to satisfy too many different segments will fail because in trying to serve the varied needs of many different markets, it will, by definition, be suboptimal for any one specific segment and uncompetitive relative to a more optimized solution. Segmentation means saying no to potential customers and revenue and as a result is often a difficult task for a Product Manager. However, by being focused on one or a small number of attractive market segments, the overall product, including features, messaging, and marketing, will be much more targeted, thereby increasing the probability of success.*

## Define the overall market (TAM).

Start by identifying the overall market to be segmented. This is often called the Total Addressable Market or TAM. TAM is more easily defined for existing products and their derivatives and can be challenging to define for new-to-the-world products. For the latter, an existing or historical market could be used as an initial proxy. Calculate the overall market size by multiplying the estimated total number of customers by an estimated average selling price (ASP).

## Identify the "bases" for segmentation.

Consider and identify the best way to divide the overall market into different segments such that each segment shares common needs or wants that make them materially different from other segments. Common segmentation bases include:

- **Demographic** – Age, gender, education, occupation, income, etc.
- **Geographic** – Location including country, region, etc.
- **Psychographic** – Personality, lifestyle, opinions, and values.
- **Firmographic** – (Common in B2B) Industry type, company size, location, strategic importance, etc.
- **Behavioral** – Product usage, preference, choices, price-sensitivity, quality-sensitivity, service-sensitivity, benefits sought, etc.

## Select one or more target segments (SAM).

Once the overall market has been segmented, select one or more segments as the focus of the product and marketing efforts. First, decide on the number of segments that will be selected. This is usually one or two but not more. Next, decide on the criteria for selecting the segment. Common criteria for segment selection include:

- Segment size
- Segment growth
- Buyer and supplier power
- Competition, current and future
- Defensibility
- Strategic alignment
- Alignment with core competencies

A segment is viable if it allows you to identify and reach target customers, if it's stable over the lifetime of the product, and if it's large enough to be profitable. The selected segment or segments is the Serviceable Available Market (SAM), or the portion of TAM that will be targeted by the product.

## Estimate Share of Market (SOM).

At the end of the market segmentation exercise, estimate the portion of SAM that the product aspires to capture. This is the Share of Market, which is a portion of SAM. Outline the justification for the anticipated SOM.

# 26

# POSITIONING

*There is a limit to the number of things each of us can hold in our minds, and this is equally true for the target customers of your product. For any given job your customer is trying to get done, there is a finite number of solutions they are aware of and one best solution that occupies that "slot" in their mind. The goal of positioning is to place your product as the best solution for the specific job in the customer's mind so when they go to do that job again, they choose your product. Therefore, positioning is the perception you want to create for your product. Positioning is created using various proof-points including key product features, marketing messages and channels, pricing, and commentary from key market influencers.*

**Define the target market.**
Identify the target market for the product and the archetypal target customer(s). Leverage prior work on market segmentation and in writing customer personas if those exist.

**List the needs and wants of the target market.**
Examine the key needs and wants for the target market. What jobs are the target customers trying to get done? Again, leverage the work done defining product requirements to assist with this part of the analysis. Some markets have multiple key "customers" including the end-user, the economic buyer, or other key influencers. Positioning should be created for each key target "customer" since they will have unique needs and therefore the positioning will be different for each. List the important purchase or selection criteria for each type of target customer and prioritize them.

**Research competitor's positioning.**
Compare the target customer purchase or selection criteria against current competitive offerings and identify how competitors are positioning themselves in the market.

**Identify the product's competitive advantage.**
Compare your product to competitor offerings on the key purchase or selection criteria. Use a table or create a "positioning map," typically a two-by-two matrix comparing products across two key criteria. Identify where your product has a competitive advantage in key purchase or selection criteria.

**Decide on the positioning strategy.**
Positioning can be established in a number of different ways. Decide which is best given the customers' needs and wants, the competitor's positioning, and your competitive advantage. Positioning can be:

- Against a competitor
- Within a product category
- For specific users

Or based on:

- A product benefit
- A product attribute
- A usage occasion
- Price

**Create a positioning statement.**
Write a positioning statement using the following template:

*For [target customer] that [key need or purchase criteria]*
*[product name] is a [product category]*
*that [key reason to purchase].*
*Unlike [key competitor], [product name] is*
*[key differentiator].*

**Determine how the proposed positioning will be realized.**
Given the proposed positioning, consider the most important ways the positioning can be made real. Key things to consider are:

- Key product features to emphasize in support of the positioning.
- How packaging reinforces the positioning.
- How pricing will establish and reinforce the positioning.
- The key marketing messages that will best communicate the positioning.
- The best marketing channels to reach the target customer with the marketing message.
- How key market influencers can help create and reinforce the positioning.

# 27

# PRODUCT MESSAGING

*Messaging is the key information you convey about the product to target audiences.*

**Define the target audiences.**
Identify each of the key audiences for which messaging is needed. For example, this could include end-users, buyers, and industry analysts.

**Identify key points to communicate with each audience.**
List the top three things to communicate to each audience. For the end-user, this could focus on key product benefits whereas a business-to-business purchaser may be more interested in the total cost of ownership and warranty.

**Review the brand voice.**
If you have corporate brand voice guidelines, review those to ensure product messaging is on-brand and consistent with the brand voice. This can also include messaging restrictions provided by Corporate Marketing.

**Create the messaging for each audience.**
Create compelling messaging to communicate the key points to each target audience.

**Identify evidence in support of the key messages.**
Identify and list key evidence or data-points that can be used to support the key claims in the product messaging.

**Identify and create other key messaging-related deliverables.**
In addition to key messages, other common messaging-related deliverables include:

- **The Value Proposition** – A brief statement summarizing what makes the product different from and better than the competition.
- **A marketing tagline** – A catchphrase or slogan for the product that summarizes the product benefits.
- **An elevator pitch** – A very short (20-60 seconds) summary of the product, typically intended to generate interest in the product.
- **Summary statements** – Short descriptions of the product varying in length and detail.

# 28

# LAUNCH PREPARATION

*Product launch marks the debut of the new product in the market and is a critical milestone in the new product life cycle. The product launch is the opportunity to create a positive first impression and to set out the value proposition, positioning, and competitive differentiation of the product. Initial awareness and demand for the product are created during the product launch. Launch planning and preparation start early in the planning phase of the new product process and continue throughout development.*

## Define launch goals and metrics.

Identify the most important goals for the product launch. These can include goals for customer awareness, customer evaluation of the product, number of leads, number of positive reviews, etc. Review the goals with key stakeholders to gather feedback and ensure alignment. Define metrics to measure success and determine the return on investment for the product launch.

## Decide on the launch timing and location.

Decide on the optimal launch timing and the ideal launch location. Sometimes a product will be announced at a time before being made available to purchase and other times a "soft launch" is used as a precursor or trial run of the full launch activity. Common launch venues include public or trade events, private events, or a website.

## Close on the budget.

Estimate the necessary budget for launch and secure budget approval.

## Confirm launch readiness.

Product launches typically carry significant expense and launching a product that is not ready can have a disastrous effect on the company. It's the responsibility of the Product Manager to determine whether to launch the product or not. Sometimes the right decision is not to launch the product, as painful as that might be, and to go back and fix some critical aspect of the product to make it truly launch-ready. Create a launch readiness checklist during the planning phase of the new product process and finalize it during final launch preparation. Key areas to address in the checklist include the following:

- **Product readiness.** The necessary features are properly developed and tested and are ready to be put in the hands of customers.
- **Operational readiness.** The organization is ready to support the manufacturing, marketing, sale, and support of the product.
    - Sales team readiness: The Sales team compensation structure is updated to accommodate the new product, and the Sales and support team are trained on the product.
    - Marketing readiness: A marketing communications plan has been created. The optimal communications channels have been identified (traditional, email, web, and social media) and the assets needed to best communicate the product messaging to the target audiences are in place (brochures, presentations, videos, demos, etc.). Any necessary PR activity has been planned including pre-launch press briefings, partner co-announcements, and press releases.
    - Operational readiness: Sufficient product is in the channel to service early demand, operational processes and systems have been set up to support the product, and the product is orderable.
- **Costs and pricing.** The economics of the business case have been revalidated, and the product still makes economic sense.
- **Demand.** Demand for the product still exists, and nothing has shifted in the market to dampen demand materially.
- **The competitive landscape.** Competitors have not made changes to their offering that negatively alter the product's differentiation.

# 29

# POST-LAUNCH RETROSPECTIVE

*A retrospective is a look back at the results of a project or a phase of a project to identify opportunities for future improvement. A retrospective can be conducted at different stages throughout the new product process. This section discusses a post-launch retrospective meeting, where a team of stakeholders meets and reviews how the overall project went now that the product is finally in the market and the team has had the opportunity to reflect upon the new product project.*

## Define the agenda for the retrospective.

A generic agenda for a retrospective meeting is:

- What went well?
- What didn't go well and why?
- What can be done differently next time?

Define an agenda for the retrospective meeting that is customized to the specific project. Often the meeting will focus on specific areas while still addressing the above three key questions. Common areas to discuss include:

- **Scope.** Was the product scope clear? Was there scope creep?
- **Schedule.** Was the project schedule realistic? Did the project meet the schedule? What caused schedule slips and how can these be avoided in future projects?
- **Launch timing.** Was the launch timing appropriate for the product?
- **Budget.** Was the project, including the launch effort, within budget?
- **Launch goals and metrics.** Was the launch successful? Did the team achieve the launch goals?

- **Sales goals.** Is the product selling as expected?
- **Sales Enablement.** Was Sales Enablement delivered as planned? Is it being used? Is it effective?
- **Risk management.** Was risk management successful?
- **Training and support.** Was product training completed successfully? Is the support process working as expected?

## Identify the optimal time for the retrospective meeting.

Schedule the retrospective meeting long enough after the launch that the team has had time to understand and reflect upon the project, but soon enough that important details are easily remembered.

## Identify the required attendees.

Ideally, all key stakeholders that worked on the product should attend. Common attendees include:

- Product Manager
- Program or Project Manager
- Engineering management including Development and QA
- Sales Representative
- Marketing Representative
- Customer Support Representative
- Manufacturing Representative
- Finance Representative

## Send a questionnaire to attendees before the retrospective meeting.

A questionnaire is a useful tool to gather input from all attendees before the meeting. This can often be done using an email or online survey. A questionnaire gives all stakeholders an opportunity to provide feedback. For the retrospective meeting organizer, the responses can be used to identify key topics that would benefit from discussion at the retrospective meeting.

## Hold the retrospective meeting.

Finalize the agenda at the beginning of the meeting and then work on identifying what went well, what didn't, and what actions will be taken to improve in the future. Capture and share the lessons and follow-up to ensure that proposed changes and improvements will be implemented.

# 30

# MARKETING PLAN

*The Marketing Plan defines the marketing goals for the product throughout the product life cycle. The Marketing Plan is usually created and owned by the Marketing department, but since marketing is critical to the product's commercial success, the Product Manager has a vested interest in ensuring the Marketing Plan is properly created and executed. The Product Manager closely collaborates with the Marketing staff that creates and executes the Marketing Plan and the Product Manager typically provides key input to the Marketing Plan and reviews the plan before it's finalized.*

**Review the business unit and product line Marketing Plans.**
An individual product is often part of a wider product line and part of a portfolio of products offered by a corporate division or business unit. If Marketing Plans are available at these levels, review the plans to ensure the Marketing Plan for the product supports and aligns with these plans.

**Review Marketing Plans for the prior versions of the product.**
If the product is the next generation of an existing product, review the Marketing Plans for prior versions of the product to understand the marketing goals and marketing activities for those versions and consider how those could apply to the new product. If possible, find out where the prior plans were successful and where they could have been improved and how that learning can be applied to the Marketing Plan for the new product.

**Align with Marketing on the goals and strategy for the product, especially the target market.**
Spend time with the Marketing staff that will contribute to, and create, the overall Marketing Plan to ensure they understand the overall product strategy and the

rationale for the high-level product goals. Discuss all elements of the Marketing Mix, the value proposition, positioning, messaging, and revenue forecasts. Pay particular attention to ensure there is a deep shared understanding of the target market and target customers since these are central to the Marketing Plan.

**Map out the "customer journey" and identify where marketing support is needed.**

Identify the different stages of the customer journey for each different type of "customer" (for example, there could be a target "end user" that is different to the "purchaser," and there may be other key "influencers" that each have their own customer journey). A generic customer journey maps the steps from when the customer becomes aware of a need, through purchase and after purchase. Use stages that best reflect the actual steps a customer goes through for the given product. Identify how marketing can help at each stage of the customer journey.

**Identify marketing goals in support of the overall product goals.**

Specify the overall marketing goals for the product given the product strategy and goals. The marketing goals should be high-level and are used to guide the various marketing activities and programs. High-level marketing goals often relate to creating some specified level of awareness and demand for the product over a given timeframe.

**Create the Marketing Plan.**

Build plans for the different parts of the overall marketing effort in support of the high-level marketing goals considering the customer journey. Areas to consider include:

- Advertising
- Social media
- Direct mail and email marketing
- Public Relations including media and influencer outreach
- Events
- Sales Enablement
- Training programs

**Close on the timing of marketing activity.**

Create an overall marketing schedule with the timing of key events and marketing activities to ensure alignment across the different sub-plans.

**Secure the marketing budget.**
Define the necessary budget and gain approval for the budget.

**Define metrics to measure progress and success.**
Identify metrics to measure each marketing program and to determine the return on investment (RoI), and, ultimately determine if the marketing efforts are successful.

**Monitor execution of the plan through the product life cycle and course-correct as needed.**
Monitor the ongoing marketing activity and make changes as needed to ensure the product and marketing goals are being achieved. Revisit and update the Marketing Plan as the product moves through the product life cycle, from introduction through growth, maturity, and decline, and as the need for marketing and the types of marketing evolve.

# 31

# SALES ENABLEMENT

*Sales Enablement is the product information, assets, tools, and processes used to empower the Sales organization to sell the product. Although the Sales and Marketing organization often own Sales Enablement, the Product Manager typically plays a key role in ensuring the optimal Sales Enablement is defined and delivered. A deficit in Sales Enablement will have a direct negative impact on the Product Manager as they will become overly involved in the Sales process. Most often, this is not scalable, and the Product Manager will then become a bottleneck. By creating a great Sales Enablement process and package, the Product Manager can help empower the Sales organization to independently drive the sales process and maximize the revenue opportunity for the product.*

**Understand the sales process for the product.**
Work with the Sales organization to understand the different stages of the sales pipeline and what is needed to engage at each stage successfully. A generic sales pipeline has prospects, leads, and customers. Consider what it takes to engage prospects and turn them into leads and likewise what it takes to convert leads into customers and then drive repeat purchase. When doing this, have a "buyer perspective": Think about what the buyer needs to move through the sales pipeline. Visit buyers of prior versions of the product to understand why they bought and what influenced their purchase decision.

**Review Sales Enablement for existing products.**
Review the Sales Enablement for existing products and discuss with the Sales organization what has worked well and what could be improved.

## Define and deliver the Sales Enablement.

Given the insight gathered on the sales pipeline process, define and deliver the optimal Sales Enablement. Typically, the Sales and Marketing organization owns Sales Enablement, but the Product Manager is a key stakeholder in the definition and delivery process. A key consideration is how Sales Enablement assets and collateral will be stored and made available to the Sales team. If the Sales team cannot easily find a piece of collateral or know whether it's the latest version, they will inundate the Product Manager with requests. Items to consider as part of Sales Enablement include:

- Training on the product and the support process
- Qualification criteria to determine if a prospect is a good target
- Product name, branding, and messaging information
- Product presentations
- Datasheets
- A one-page product summary
- Technical whitepapers
- Sales scripts
- Email templates
- Social media messages
- Blog posts
- Product demos and demo scripts
- Customer success case studies
- Competitor comparisons and competitor selling collateral
- Overcoming common barriers to adoption
- Pricing and information on justifying the price
- FAQ (Frequently Asked Questions)

## Monitor usage of Sales Enablement throughout the product life cycle.

It's important to ensure that Sales Enablement is effective. Ideally, the usage of each piece of collateral is measured and reviewed. If an item is underutilized, the Product Manager should work with the Sales and Marketing organization to understand why and to make any necessary changes. Likewise, the Product Manager should periodically enquire about gaps in the Sales Enablement and bridge those gaps with new enablement assets and processes. Monitoring of the Sales Enablement is particularly important in the time immediately after launch, so issues and gaps can be identified and addressed early in the product life cycle.

# 32

# PRODUCT TRAINING

*A Product Manager is often called upon to create or help create training for a new product and to deliver that training. Training is a common activity around a product launch or when the product changes. The audience for training could be internal or external and can cover a wide array of topics.*

## Define the audience.

Specify the audience for the training. Is the audience internal to the company or external? Common internal audiences include Sales, Marketing, Support, Operations, Legal, and Finance, and common external audiences include customers, partners, analysts, and media. Also, consider the audience's location and how training may need to be localized.

## Identify the training objective.

Define the training objective given the audience. For example, the objective could be to ensure product understanding or to equip the Sales team to determine customer qualification.

## Define a success metric.

Based on the objective, identify a measure of success and plan to measure the success of the training after completion.

## Detail the training curriculum.

Given the target audience, the audience location, and the training objective, define the optimal curriculum for the training. Common areas include:

- The customer and their needs
- Customer qualification

- Naming and branding
- Features and benefits
- Positioning
- Value proposition
- Messaging
- Product demonstration
- Sales Enablement overview
- Support processes
- Pricing
- Competitive analysis and how to win
- Overcoming customer concerns
- Roadmap
- End-of-life and support plans for prior versions of the product
- Case studies

## Deliver the training and measure success.

Deliver the training and measure the success relative to the training objective using the success metrics. Monitor the need for ongoing or "refresher training."

# 33

# PRODUCT DEMOS

*Demonstrating product features and benefits is a key skill for successful product management. Often, the Product Manager will conduct the demo, and at other times, the Product Manager will define demos for others to carry out. Demos are likely required in the early stages of the new product process to gain support for the new concept. During development and testing, you can use demos to showcase recent work and get feedback, either from internal stakeholders or customers. Demos to potential and existing customers are a critical part of the sales process for winning new business and are also often an integral part of tradeshows and other events featuring the product.*

**Define the demo goal.**
Consider the purpose of the demo. Is it to move a "prospect" to the next stage of the sales funnel by persuading them of key benefits of the product? Or is it to gain feedback on a proposed feature during development?

**Consider the audience.**
Think about the audience's needs. What needs, wants, or goals do they have that the product can help achieve? Engage directly with the audience or with the demo organizer to confirm your understanding of the audience's need before defining the optimal demo.

**Understand key constraints.**
Enquire about and confirm all potential constraints for the demo. These include how much time is allocated for the demo, the characteristics of the location (is the demo to happen in a small office space or a large, noisy tradeshow floor?), and the size of the audience.

### Review notes from prior demos.

Keep notes on prior demos indicating what went well to determine what should be repeated and what could be improved. Integrate any learnings that are relevant to the demo at hand.

### Define the demo.

Given your agenda for the demo ("your goal") and the audience's agenda ("their goal"), define the best demo that will accomplish both. Items to consider when defining the demo include:

- An "A/B" demo is often very effective where you show the audience today's solution ("A") and then contrast that with the new product ("B") and how it is superior.
- Plan to start with the high-level context before driving down into the details.
- Consider localization and cultural sensitivities when doing demos for foreign audiences.
- Consider what could go wrong and how you will respond if something does go awry.
- Plan to end the demo with a call to action in support of the goal for the demo.

### Do a dry run.

Do a dry run of the demo and practice it a few times. Ideally, do the dry run in the location where the actual demo will occur using the actual equipment and leave the equipment and room set up. Confirm the actual demo meets all the constraints including timing. If possible, record a video of yourself doing the demo to identify areas for improvement.

### Confirm the agenda at the start of the demo.

Spend a short time at the beginning of the demo in a conversation with the audience to confirm your understanding of "their goal." Be prepared to pivot on the fly if you find out new information during that discovery process.

### Deliver the demo.

Again, present the demo as a conversation with the audience on their needs and goals and show how the product can help them. Speak in terms of their agenda and using their vernacular. Keep within the allotted time.

**Conduct a postmortem within one hour.**

Do a quick postmortem shortly after the end of the demo while the experience is still fresh in your mind. Identify what went well and should be continued in future demos and what could be improved next time. Write down your notes for review as part of your next demo preparation.

# 34

# PRESENTATIONS

*Product Managers spend much of their time communicating on topics including market trends, customers, competitors, the product vision and product strategy, the value proposition, schedule and milestones, pricing, and a myriad of other topics related to the product. A key communication skill for successful product management is the ability to give presentations to both internal and external audiences.*

## Consider the audience.

Before creating any presentation material, consider the audience and their reason for attending the presentation:

- Who is the audience?
- How many attendees are expected?
- What is the audience's background?
- Why is the audience in attendance and how does that affect the presentation? For example, an audience may be required to attend, they may want to learn something, or they could have some need they hope the product will satisfy.
- What does the audience expect from the presentation?
- What do you want the audience to do after the presentation, the "call to action"?

## Understand key constraints.

Now that the audience has been understood, identify any key constraints for the presentation. These include:

- **Time allocation** – How much time is available for the presentation? Does time need to be allocated to questions and discussion? Plan on using only 80% of the time to allow some margin for eventualities such as the prior presenter going over or questions and answers taking longer than anticipated.
- **Time of the day** – When will the presentation occur and what is the impact of that on the presentation? For example, the audience will likely be tired at the end of the day.
- **Venue** – What is the venue like? Is it a small or large area? How will that affect the presentation?

### Define a headline for the presentation.

Create a one-sentence statement for the central point of the presentation. This should be the one thing you would want the audience to remember or do.

### Brainstorm key points.

On paper or a whiteboard, brainstorm all ideas and points you may want to make in the presentation in support of the central theme or headline. Group points until you have no more than three key points. Make the key points as concise as possible.

### Link the key points into a narrative.

Determine how you will link the three key points together into a narrative that will become the basis for the presentation. Consider what evidence you will use to reinforce your key points including statistics and stories. Add drama to the narrative by creating tension and release, for example, by asking and answering a question. Determine how to connect on both an emotional and intellectual level with the audience. Plan for a strong opening and finishing on a high note. A general outline for a presentation is:

- State the headline.
- List the key points.
- Revisit the key points and explain each in more detail.
- Restate the key points and close with the key takeaway or call to action.

### Create the presentation material.

Taking the audience, constraints, and narrative into account, determine the best medium for delivering the presentation including slides, videos, exhibits, handouts, or simply speaking with or without notes. If presentation slides are needed, here are some key considerations:

- Think about the best way to convey each key point using images, charts, videos, text, etc.
- Use visuals to reinforce your words, not repeat them.
- Use text and bullet points sparingly and only as a last resort after considering other options. Limit words to no more than five per slide.
- Create handouts to convey lots of text, data, or complex charts.
- Avoid distracting slide transitions or animations.
- Remove anything extraneous on the slides.

**Prepare to deliver the presentation.**

Forget about perfection and trying to memorize the whole presentation. Instead, focus on becoming so familiar with the key points of the material that you remember to cover each of them as intended and your presentation style comes across to the audience as natural. The most important preparation step is to practice the presentation several times so that when you come to deliver it you only need to refer to your material a minimal amount. The key preparation steps are as follows:

- Practice speaking out loud.
- Ideally, practice in the presentation location or a room or space like the actual presentation location.
- Pay attention to transitions to ensure they're smooth and have a sense of momentum through the narrative.
- Think about ways of getting the audience involved in the presentation, for example, by asking questions, asking for a show of hands, or giving things away during the presentation.
- If you will be asked questions, consider which questions you are most likely to be asked and practice answering them.

# 35

# CUSTOMER MEETINGS

*Product Managers are often involved in customer and client meetings throughout the product life cycle. For example, the Product Manager may be seeking feedback on a new product concept or a feature during product development, and at other times the Product Manager may be assisting the Sales team in persuading a lead to adopt the product.*

**Define the meeting purpose.**
Clearly identify the business objective for the meeting. What is the desired outcome?

**Consider the customer and the meeting background.**
Research the customer history and the context for the meeting. Some things to consider include:

- Does the customer already use products from your company?
- What issues have they had with your company?
- What is their market standing and what recent successes or challenges have they encountered?
- What are the customer's business priorities?
- Review the potential customer attendees and identify their agenda and whether they are pro, neutral, or negative relative to your company or product.
- Review recent communications between the customer and your company.

### Create a meeting agenda.

Given the meeting objective and the customer background, create an agenda for the meeting. What key topics need to be covered and what is the best way to cover them? Identify any presentation material, demos, or other assets that are needed to cover the agenda.

### Decide on attendees.

Given the agenda, identify who needs to attend from your company. The minimum necessary attendees should be invited to cover the agenda. Identify the names and titles of the attendees from the customer side.

### Confirm the agenda.

Confirm the agenda and attendees with the customer to ensure alignment. Make any final changes.

### Close on logistics.

Finalize all logistics including where and when the meeting will occur, the allotted time, travel logistics to and from the meeting location, etc.

### Create the meeting material.

Create the necessary presentation material, product demos, pre-reading, and other items needed to cover the agenda.

### Prepare for likely questions.

Consider questions that are likely to be asked by the customer and the best way of answering them including who will answer. Also, consider the questions you will ask the customer.

### Distribute pre-reading.

Send any required pre-reading material to attendees from your company and the customer.

### Distribute the meeting plan.

Create a one-page summary of the meeting plan and distribute it to all attendees from your company to ensure alignment on the meeting objectives and plan.

## Arrange an internal pre-meeting if necessary.

If the meeting is important, hold an internal pre-meeting and do a dry run. If multiple people are attending from your company, identify who will lead the meeting, who will take notes, and who will present what and when.

## Hold the meeting.

Some key considerations during the meeting include:

- Monitor how the meeting is progressing and be flexible and switch course if the meeting is not going as planned. Hold to the meeting objective but be flexible on how you get there.
- Stay focused and mindful of the time and steer the conversation if needed to stay "on agenda."
- Be sure to capture the key points from the meeting and all action items.

## Debrief.

Do a debrief after the meeting and compare the results with the meeting objective and meeting plan. Note the outcome of the meeting.

## Send meeting minutes.

Create a summary of the meeting and distribute the notes to all key stakeholders within 24 hours. The meeting summary should include:

- Customer name, date, and location of the meeting
- Name and titles of attendees, internal and customers
- Meeting outcome
- Action items, owners, and due dates
- A summary of key items covered in the meeting

## Follow-up.

Ensure that all requests and action items from the meeting are properly and promptly addressed.

# 36

# CUSTOMER NEGOTIATIONS

*Being able to negotiate successfully is a key skill for Product Managers. For example, a Product Manager typically has no direct control over the people and resources that are needed to make a product successful, and therefore the Product Manager needs to use indirect influence and negotiation to advance the cause of the product. While a product is being actively sold, a Product Manager is often part of the team that facilitates important customer negotiations. The key steps in conducting a customer negotiation are outlined below although this general approach can be leveraged for any negotiation.*

## Define your negotiation position.

Spend time with the deal team and other stakeholders to discuss your company's priorities in the deal and gain alignment on the following constraints for the negotiation.

- **Interests:** List all items that are important to your company and prioritize them.
- **Resistance Point:** Identify the "bottom line" or the point beyond which you are unwilling to settle.
- **BATNA:** The Best Alternative to a Negotiated Agreement is your best alternative if a deal cannot be reached and you must walk away. Knowing your BATNA helps prevent settling for terms that are worse than your best alternative. The BATNA is often the same as the Resistance Point but not always.
- **Aspiration Point:** Your Aspiration Point is the best deal you could hope to achieve realistically. A "good" deal is one that is better than your BATNA, more than the Resistance Point, and as close to the Aspiration Point as possible.

### Consider the customer's position.

Identify and discuss the things that are likely to be of value to the customer and attempt to prioritize them. Estimate their Resistance Point, BATNA, and Aspiration Point.

### Identify the "Bargaining Zone."

The Bargaining Zone or Zone of Possible Agreement (ZOPA) is the range within which you and the customer can reach an agreement. This zone is usually bounded by the two parties' Resistance Points.

### Strategize on how to "expand the pie."

Spend time before the negotiation considering how you can "expand the pie" and offer more value to the customer given their interests. Often there are things of value to the customer that may be easy to give in exchange for things of value to you, for example, timing concessions, warranty, audit rights, marketing development support, and bundling with other products. Ideally, engage the other party before the negotiation to confirm your understanding.

### Prepare an opening offer.

Having done the research, prepare an opening offer. By making the first move, you will be able to set the expectations and tone for the negotiation and anchor the discussion. Define the opening offer and the rationale you will use to justify the offer. Have a perspective of offering a deal that meets the interests of both parties and is above both parties' Resistance Points.

### Plan concessions.

Consider the concessions the deal team is willing to make in pursuit of an agreement including the timing and rationale for the concessions. Practice "Give/Get" negotiation where if you give up something, you ask for something of equal value in return.

### Plan for and conduct the negotiation.

Working with the deal team, create a plan for conducting the negotiation.

- Plan to open the negotiation by identifying common ground and common goals.
- Share details of your interests and enquire about the customer's interests.

Ask questions to seek to confirm your understanding of their position (Resistance Point, Aspiration Point, etc.).

- Look to expand the pie. Based on the preparation work, probe to see if the items you identified that may be of value to the other party are indeed valuable.
- Summarize and confirm your understanding of both parties' positions.
- Make the opening offer and provide the rationale.
- Negotiate with a perspective of focusing on common goals, problem-solving, and striving toward your Aspiration Point and a position more than your Resistance Point.

**Debrief after the negotiation is complete.**

Debrief with the deal team. Identify what went well, what didn't, and what you will do differently the next time.

# 37

# MEDIA INTERVIEWS

*Product Managers are often called upon to meet with members of the media during a product launch, as a company spokesperson at tradeshows and other events, or when assisting partners in their media efforts. Fundamental skills related to interacting with the media include message development and delivery and general interview preparation. Often the Product Manager is supported by an internal PR department or external PR firm for media interviews and events.*

**Understand the context.**
Work with the PR team arranging the interview or event to understand the background, context, and goals for the interview or event. Read all the briefing material. Identify and discuss the type of story you have, for example, a new product, breaking news, or commentary on some industry trend.

**Define the objective.**
What is the overall objective of the event or interview?

**Research the media participants and their audience.**
Ideally, PR will provide biographies of the media participants and a summary of relevant recent coverage but, if not, spend time doing your own research. Pay attention to the reporter's target audience to understand who they are and why they would be interested in this news story. Understand the reporter's style and whether they are pro, neutral, or negative relative to your company or the topic at hand.

**Develop the story.**

Identify three key messages that best communicate the main theme and support the interview objective. Messages should be short and focused on the target audience. Identify ways of supporting your message including statistics and short stories.

**Identify likely objections and questions.**

Consider questions reporters are likely to ask and how best to answer them.

**Do a dry run.**

Work with a member of the PR team to do a dry run.

- Practice delivering the key messages and make refinements as necessary. Focus on always bridging back to the key messages during the interview. Practice using verbal cues (for example, "The key thing to remember is...") and non-verbal cues (for example, using gestures) to draw attention to the key messages.
- Practice answering likely questions and refine the answers as necessary.
- Have the interviewer practice common reporter techniques such as using easy questions followed by more difficult questions, silence, creating controversy, using hostile questions, and using interruptions.

**Confirm logistics.**

Confirm where and when the event or interview will occur, contact information for members of the PR team, etc. Confirm and prepare the appropriate attire for the event.

**Do final preparation.**

Mentally rehearse and do the final preparation for the interview. Key things to consider relative to the interview include the following.

- Speak decisively and avoid filler language.
- Avoid technical jargon.
- Clarify a question if you don't understand it.
- Nothing is "off the record."
- Set the record straight if reporters bring up inaccurate information.

- Always be truthful. Defer if you don't know the answer to a question.
- If something comes up that cannot be discussed, have a quick response prepared, such as "Nothing to announce at this time."
- Keep answers short.
- Be positive and show interest.

# END-OF-LIFE

# 38

# DECIDING TO RETIRE A PRODUCT

*Deciding to end-of-life (EOL) a product is an important yet often neglected decision for a Product Manager. Products often continue in the market long after they should have been retired and while most companies have formal new product processes for defining and launching new products, many do not have the same discipline when deciding to end-of-life products.*

## Consider the product and category life cycle.

Consider where the product is in its life cycle and the product category life cycle. Products and product categories in the decline phase of the life cycle are often candidates for end-of-life. Also, the decision to develop the next generation of a product should trigger end-of-life consideration for the old version of the product.

## Compare the product portfolio to the product strategy.

Compare the product or product portfolio to the company, business unit, and product line strategy. Does each product continue to make sense relative to the strategic goals of the business? Does the product continue to align with, and leverage, the core competencies and skills of the company? If not, then an end-of-life decision should be considered.

## Monitor redundancy in the product portfolio.

Periodically, review the overall product portfolio and look for areas of overlap and redundancy. Are there too many products in the portfolio?

## Conduct a competitive and market analysis.

When doing competitive and market analysis, consider how changes in the market either in customer preferences, competitive solutions, or technology advancements could make current products obsolete in the future and consider whether an end-of-life decision is reasonable. Often it takes years to fully retire a product and getting ahead of the process can save considerable resources.

### Monitor revenue, unit volume, profitability, and market share.

Revenue, unit shipments, profitability, and market share should be actively monitored both in the absolute sense and regarding trends over time as potential triggers for an end-of-life decision. When a product enters the maturity and decline phase of the life cycle, revenue growth slows and ultimately declines. Profitability can turn negative even during the maturity phase depending on market conditions. Once a product no longer makes economic sense, it should be actively reviewed for retirement.

### Build an end-of-life decision process.

If your company or business unit does not have an end-of-life decision process, create one. Establish an agreed upon set of rules to guide the end-of-life process. Identify conditions that trigger an end-of-life decision. Establish an end-of-life committee of key stakeholders to assist in the decision-making process.

# 39

# END-OF-LIFE PLAN

*A product or business can be "sunset" in several different ways. Sometimes a product, product line, or business continues to make economic sense in isolation but no longer aligns with the corporate strategy. In this instance, the product or business could be sold to a different company or set up as an independent entity. Elements of a product such as intellectual property can likewise be carved out and sold to a third party. The more common case of the full discontinuance of a single product is discussed in this section with steps on creating and executing the end-of-life plan.*

## Form an end-of-life team.

Consider the functional groups that the end-of-life will affect including Sales, Marketing, Operations, Support, Finance, and Legal, and form a team with representatives of each that will work on the creation and execution of the end-of-life plan. Having members of the key functional groups participate on the team will ensure that all important items are included and planned for, helping to drive internal alignment in the process.

## Create the end-of-life plan.

The end-of-life plan should consider and address the following:

- **Portfolio impact:** What is the impact on the overall product portfolio of discontinuing the product? Are there other products that depend on the end-of-life product? If so, how will those dependencies be addressed?
- **Replacement strategy:** What alternative will be offered to customers?
- **End-of-sale and service:** How long will the product and related spare parts

continue to be sold? How long will the product be supported, including things like bug fixes for software products?

- **Inventory and returns:** For physical goods, how will inventory of finished goods and spare parts be addressed both before the end-of-life and after? How will returns be handled?
- **Price:** Are changes to the product pricing required given the end-of-life? For example, pricing can be used to encourage sales of inventory or to motivate customers to move to a next version of the product.
- **Legal:** Review all customer contracts to understand contractual commitments that could impact the end-of-life. Plan for stopping new contracts and making any necessary legal communications.
- **Milestones and schedule:** Define key milestones including internal and external communications, end-of-sale, and end-of-support.
- **Communications:** Identify all key internal and external stakeholders and create a plan for key communications to all parties. Plan to discuss the end-of-life with key internal stakeholders first and gain alignment on the plan. Create a "discontinuation notice" for external parties, including customers and channel partners, and have that reviewed by internal stakeholders.

### Execute the end-of-life plan.

Execute the end-of-life plan through the cross-functional team. The key goals are to ensure the product is retired appropriately and that customers and partners are properly supported through the process. Internally, the team should communicate with all key stakeholders, gain alignment on the plan, and ensure each functional group completes the things they need to do. Externally, the end-of-life is communicated to customers, usually in a coordinated way with the Sales, Operations, and Legal teams. The end-of-life team continues to meet and work the plan through all key milestones including end-of-sale and end-of-support.

# MANAGING PRODUCT MANAGERS

# 40

# RECRUITING

*The most important parts of a manager's role are recruiting, developing, and retaining high-performance product team members. This section outlines general steps for hiring Product Managers.*

**Define the role.**

Consider the role including the key duties and competencies for the Product Manager. Define the role as it exists currently and consider how the role is expected to evolve. Create a job description.

**Create a hiring plan.**

Meet with key stakeholders including your manager, the HR partner, and recruiter and discuss the hiring process. Determine how candidate sourcing, screening, and interviewing will happen and by whom. Review how the hiring decision will be made. Identify key activities, owners, and timelines, and document the plan.

**Search for and recruit potential candidates.**

Post the job description on the company job website and external job posting sites and promote the opening. Often, the best Product Managers are not actively looking for a new job, so a key part of the hiring process is to find and recruit these high performers. Leverage your network internal and external to the company and ask for recommendations on candidates. Work with the recruiter to identify companies, universities, and geographic regions where good candidates may be located and have the recruiter conduct a search.

**Do an initial screening.**

Using the job description and other information on the role and ideal candidate, create criteria to filter out resumes and to use in the initial round of screening. Screen candidates over the telephone or on a video call. The recruiter should do a very brief initial screening to confirm the details of the candidate's résumé and background. Next, the hiring manager usually does a 30-minute screening.

## Arrange and conduct the interview.

Bring candidates that pass the initial screening onsite for a day of interviews. Given that product management roles have a high degree of interpersonal interaction, it's best to do the interviews in person. Candidates will usually have five to six interviews, each lasting 45 to 60 minutes, with representatives from the hiring team, the product team, and sometimes from other key stakeholders such as Sales and Marketing.

The hiring manager should take an active role in arranging the interview. Meet with interviewers before the interview to make sure the role and the ideal candidate criteria are clear and understood. Assign specific areas for each interviewer to evaluate that are critical to the role (see the list below). These assignments will help ensure all important areas are evaluated and there is no significant overlap across interviews. Discuss how each area will be evaluated and how notes from the interviews are to be captured and distributed. Common areas to evaluate for product roles include:

- Teamwork
- Influence and leadership
- Strategic thinking
- Decision-making
- Problem-solving
- Analytical skills
- Communication skills, both verbal and written
- Product design
- Market knowledge
- Technical knowledge
- Company fit and team fit

The best measure of a candidate is to evaluate the person operating as close as possible to the actual role. Hiring the candidate as a contractor for a period to work in the role would be an ideal way to assess fit. However, that's often impractical for both the candidate and the hiring manager. Focus the interview on the key responsibilities of the specific product role and how the candidate fits these criteria. This can be accomplished in a variety of ways:

- **Homework** – Get the candidate to do an assignment based on a project they will encounter in the role. For example, get the candidate to do a market and competitive analysis for a specific product and to recommend features for the next version.
- **Case study** – Leverage a case study that outlines an actual situation the candidate is likely to encounter in the role and use the case study as part of the interview process.
- **Presentation** – Given the importance of communication and influence in most product roles, have the candidate create and present on a topic related to the role.
- **Behavioral questions** – Use behavioral questions to see how the candidate would respond to common product management situations.

## Make the hiring decision.

The hiring decision is typically made either by the hiring manager or by an independent hiring committee that is made up of people who are not part of the interview team. Each interviewer should provide an overall assessment of the candidate and submit notes from the interview, either to the hiring manager or the hiring committee. Interviewers should use a common ranking scheme which could be a number with an associated meaning or some alternative ranking such as: "don't hire," "hire," or "strong hire."

## Do a background and reference check.

Conduct a background check for candidates who are approved for hiring. Do not skip the background check as it can surface issues that will be much more difficult to address after the person is hired. In addition to the formal background check, the hiring manager should speak with the candidate's references. Again, this is often ignored, but it is a useful last step to confirm the hiring decision is the right one.

## Make the offer and onboard the new hire.

Finally, have the recruiter or HR put together an offer package, working with the compensation committee. The recruiter usually presents the offer and leads any negotiation on the offer package with the candidate, consulting with HR and the hiring manager during the process. After the candidate accepts the offer, the hiring manager creates an onboarding plan to start the new hire in the role successfully.

# 41

# WRITING A JOB DESCRIPTION

*A job description or "JD" is a concise summary of a job's duties and requirements. A well-written job description results in better recruitment by aligning internal stakeholders on the role and enabling candidates to clearly understand the open position, minimizing wasted cycles with unqualified candidates. Outside of recruiting, the job description is an important performance management tool since it sets the baseline against which performance is measured. Job descriptions are also useful in organizational and succession planning.*

## Title.

Use a job title that is specific, easy to understand for people outside of the company, and can be easily compared to similar jobs in the industry. The job title should communicate the ranking order with other jobs in the product organization. Example product-related job titles include:

- Associate Product Manager
- Product Manager
- Technical Product Manager
- Product Marketing Manager
- Product Owner
- Senior Product Manager
- Platform Product Manager
- Principal Product Manager
- Group Product Manager
- Director, Product Management
- VP, Product Management

- Head of Product
- SVP, Product Management
- Chief Product Officer

**Summary.**

The job summary is a brief, compelling statement of the most important parts of the role. Although the summary is usually written last, it is often the first thing a prospective candidate will read so make it a strong opening statement.

- Describe the most important responsibilities of the job.
- Show how the role fits in the wider organization.
- Sell the role and the company. Provide compelling reasons for the candidate to join, including the vision for the company and the product.

**Duties and responsibilities.**

This section is the core of the job description and includes a list of the key responsibilities and duties of the role—the work that needs to be performed and for what the Product Manager will be accountable. Descriptions should be short, start with an action verb, and focus on the desired outcome or result. List only the *key* duties of the role and don't include an exhaustive list. Example job duties for a Product Manager may include:

- Oversees the success of one or more products. Manages the products through the full product life cycle, from concept to end-of-life.
- Serves as an expert on the product and market, including customers and competitors.
- Sources attractive new product opportunities including evolutions of existing products as well as new-to-the-company products. Leads the validation of new product concepts.
- Defines the product vision and strategy. Oversees the planning for new products and owns the Product Roadmap. Builds support for the product strategy with key internal stakeholders.
- Engages the target market to understand customers' needs and wants. Defines product requirements and oversees the development of the product with the new product team.
- Understands the value of the product to customers and their willingness to pay. Sets the pricing strategy and policy.

- Introduces and markets new products and creates integrated plans with Marketing, Sales, and Operations to support launches and ongoing marketing.
- Understands the sales process for the product, arranges Sales Enablement, and supports the Sales team in customer engagements and negotiations.
- Conducts product training, product demos, and product presentations and is a spokesperson for the product at media events and tradeshows.

**Requirements and preferences.**
Requirements are "must have" qualities to get the job whereas preferences are "nice to have" traits where there is some flexibility. Delineate between the two when writing this section. Keep the list short and concise, and focus on the key items. Requirements and preferences include:

- Experience
- Competencies
- Education, training, and certifications

**Other information.**
Depending on the role, you may need to include other information, such as:

- Reporting relationships
- Summary of the key benefits, especially benefits unique to the role or company
- Salary information, which is usually not included but if it is, it's typically represented as a salary range
- Travel requirements, both domestic and international

**Legal review.**
Before publishing the job description, have it reviewed to ensure compliance with labor law including anti-discrimination laws.

# 42

# ONBOARDING

*Onboarding is the process of integrating a new employee into the team and providing them with the information, tools, and training they need to be successful in the new role. Most companies have an established process for employee onboarding. This section covers the most important steps.*

## Create an onboarding plan.

Document what the employee will do over three time periods: the first week, the first month, and the first quarter. Often, the new employee will shadow the manager and team members to observe how key aspects of the job are done. The new employee can take on smaller tasks at first and build to more complicated assignments and autonomy during the first 90 days. Consider these areas in the onboarding plan:

- **Onboarding logistics**
  - Completing the new employee orientation.
  - Reviewing company-level material such as the employee handbook.
  - Accessing key company IT systems and tools.
  - Touring the building and location.
  - Sending a hiring announcement to the organization.
- **People**
  - Understanding the team, business unit, and company organization.
  - Meeting key stakeholders including the immediate team, the product team, the management team, and other key stakeholders including Sales, Marketing, Legal, Finance, and Operations. This should be done within the first 90 days.

  - Attending key meetings including team meetings, divisional or business unit team meetings, and project team meetings.
- **Product**
  - Training on the product line and individual products including technical training and training on the product strategy, the market, and the competitive landscape.
  - Training on the new product process.
- **Goals**
  - Other specific goals for the first 90 days.

### Assign an onboarding partner.

An onboarding partner is someone other than the hiring manager who assists the new employee with onboarding. The onboarding partner should be a seasoned employee who can help the new employee in an informal, friendly way with day-to-day items that occur such as where to get lunch or where to find office supplies.

### Prepare for the new employee's first day.

Contact the employee before their start date to welcome them and discuss logistics including orientation and where and when to meet on their first day. Ensure the employee's workspace is set up and ready and that all equipment (computer, phone, etc.) and accounts (email, etc.) are prepared.

### Begin the onboarding.

Meet the new employee and review the onboarding plan. Discuss and plan how often you will meet during the first month, first 90 days, and after that. Discuss your management and working style with the employee including communication preferences. Plan an event to socialize the new employee with the team. Have the employee work through the onboarding plan and review the plan frequently together to discuss what has been completed, where there are obstacles the manager can help with, and any additions or modifications required to the plan.

# 43

# GOAL SETTING

*Goal setting is important to ensure Product Managers are focused on the most important priorities for the business, in measuring progress, and to drive personal growth. The steps in creating goals using the "OKR" framework are outlined below. OKR stands for Objectives and Key Results and is a process that defines a key business objective and a small number of metrics or key results to measure whether the business objective was accomplished. OKR is most effective when used throughout the organization as it allows OKRs to cascade from top to bottom with company OKRs leading to business unit OKRs that in turn lead to objectives for teams and individuals. The OKR framework also drives alignment and surfaces misalignment across teams and individuals that share dependencies. The steps below, written from the perspective of the team manager, focus on setting OKRs for an individual Product Manager but the process can also be used for setting goals at the team level.*

**Review prior objectives and results.**
Review the objectives for the prior planning period and the progress on key results. Also review any recent performance reviews, especially areas of underperformance that need to be addressed through OKRs for the next review period.

**Review the OKR hierarchy.**
Have each Product Manager individually review the OKRs for the company, business unit, and product line for the planning period, usually the next quarter or year. Then, bring the team together for a group discussion on those higher-level OKRs and consider how the team can best contribute to and support the company and business unit goals.

## Define objectives.

Create one-sentence qualitative statements for the key business objectives for each Product Manager. Objectives, the "O" in OKR, should focus on business outcomes and not the output or tasks to be worked on. Objectives should be short, inspiring, and stretch the Product Manager to reach for greatness but be realistic and attainable. An example objective for a Product Manager could be to: "Successfully launch version 3.0 of the mobile app at Mobile World Congress."

## Define key results to measure attainment of the business objectives.

Key results are measurable indicators of whether the objective was attained or not. Key results are quantitative, and it's typical to include three to five key results per objective. Good OKRs are specific about the desired business result but are not prescriptive on the "how," enabling the Product Manager to leverage their creativity and entrepreneurship and to figure out the best way of accomplishing the business objective. Therefore, key results should be quantitative measures of success but are not a list of tasks that must be done in support of the objective. Key results for the example objective stated above may include:

- "Achieve more than 5,000 downloads in the first week."
- "Maintain a minimum four-star rating in the app store."
- "Get product reviews published in more than 20 target publications in the first two weeks after launch."

The SMART approach to goal setting is often used to help create the KRs (Key Results) of OKRs. Key Results should be:

- **S**pecific: The result definition provides a clear description of what is to be achieved.
- **M**easurable: The result is quantifiable (for example, using a number or percentage).
- **A**chievable: The result is within the realm of possibility.
- **R**elevant: The result leads to the outcome desired by the overall OKR objective.
- **T**ime-bound: The result has a defined deadline.

### Share OKRs to ensure alignment.

One key benefit of OKRs is to ensure alignment between the Product Manager and other teams or individuals with whom the Product Manager shares dependencies. Have the Product Manager meet all stakeholders and review the OKRs and identify and address any misalignment. Where there are key dependencies between the Product Manager and other individuals, it's often best to co-write OKRs together to ensure alignment.

### Create OKRs for personal growth.

In addition to the business-focused OKRs, have the Product Manager propose OKRs to drive personal development.

### Monitor, review, and grade results.

Monitor progress throughout the year or quarter on key results and grade OKRs at the end of the review period. Hold a review session to discuss the results and identify what went well and what can be improved, and how, going forward.

# 44

# PERFORMANCE REVIEWS

*Assessing and discussing employee performance is vital to ensuring business objectives are being accomplished and that the Product Manager is improving and growing. Performance should be continually assessed, both directly by the manager and indirectly through feedback from the Product Manager and their peers. Accomplishments should be acknowledged and celebrated as they occur to reinforce the right behavior. Likewise, challenges or underperformance should be addressed immediately to prevent the impact from compounding and to get the Product Manager back on track. Regular one-on-one meetings are a great forum for discussing performance and it's common also to hold more formal performance reviews quarterly and annually, as outlined in the steps below.*

## Gather feedback on the Product Manager's performance.

Three sources of input are important on the Product Manager's performance:

- **Direct observation.** There is no substitute for direct observation by the manager on key areas of responsibility for the Product Manager. Performance should be assessed and discussed continually, and the manager should keep notes from those discussions for use later in periodic quarterly or annual reviews.
- **Self-assessment.** The manager should seek self-assessment from the Product Manager through periodic reports as well as a quarter-end or year-end self-assessment. When preparing for a formal review, the manager should also seek feedback from the Product Manager on areas outside of the immediate business objectives including what the Product Manager liked most and least about the role over the past review period, personal and career goals, and feedback on the manager's working style.

- **Multi-source assessment.** "360-degree" feedback from the Product Manager's peers and others in the organization are important to have a holistic perspective on performance.

## Evaluate the Product Manager's performance.

Consider and assess the Product Manager's performance. A good practice is to keep an up-to-date job description for the Product Manager and to use that as the baseline for performance assessment. Areas to consider when evaluating performance include:

- Goal accomplishment
- Key product management competencies such as:
    - Strategic thinking
    - Leadership
    - Influence
    - Communication
    - Teamwork
    - Market and product knowledge
- Areas where the Product Manager excelled
- Areas where the Product Manager underperformed
- Personal development and growth

## Document the assessment.

There is usually a formal review process in established companies including how feedback is captured. The performance review should be recorded and stored in the employee's file. Often, the review process requires the manager to assign a rating for overall performance as well as performance in specific areas. Assessments should be neutral, non-judgmental, and focused on how actual performance compared to the expectations of the role and progress toward business goals. Data, evidence, and specific examples should support feedback. Send the assessment to the employee the day before the review meeting, so the Product Manager has a chance to consider and respond to the assessment privately and prepare for the upcoming review meeting.

## Hold an in-person review meeting.

Arrange the meeting at least a week in advance and discuss the meeting with the Product Manager ahead of time so they know what to expect and can start preparing. Hold the meeting in a neutral location.

- Start with the positive and acknowledge where the employee met and exceeded expectations. Recognize and discuss where their strengths can continue to be leveraged in the role.
- Next, discuss any areas where the Product Manager underperformed. Feedback and discussion should focus on the business objective. Work to uncover the root cause of the underperformance (skillset, process, workload, etc.) and strategize together on how this can be addressed moving forward.
- Summarize and discuss the next steps, which should include a planning meeting to set goals for the next planning period, and to finalize a plan to address any areas of underperformance.

# 45

# TEAM DEVELOPMENT

*Developing team members to address weaknesses, enhance strengths, and grow in the discipline of product management is one of the most important parts of the manager's role and an area the manager is uniquely placed to affect.*

## Audit how much time you're spending on team development.

Although the team manager is primarily responsible for team development, many managers in product organizations are "working managers" who run the team and also make a considerable amount of individual contribution. Periodically conduct an audit to see how much time you're spending on team development and discuss that with your manager to see whether that time allocation is enough. To be effective, a manager needs to spend at least 10 percent, and ideally more, of their time on team development.

## Define the product role hierarchy.

Define each role in the product organization and have a detailed description of each role as well as the criteria required to move to each level. A typical hierarchy may include the following roles:

- Associate Product Manager
- Product Manager
- Senior Product Manager
- Director, Product Management
- VP, Product Management

Having defined criteria allows team members to understand each role and what is required to move to the next level in the organization, and provides a long-term goal to work toward when planning their career growth.

**Have a succession plan.**
Identify critical roles in the team, including the management roles, and create a plan to develop a pool of talent to be able to fill those roles over time as the need arises.

**Create a standard training curriculum.**
Identify key areas that each member of the product team should be trained on and establish a network of training providers. Training may include areas such as business strategy, pricing, finance, marketing, presentation skills, negotiation, and coding. Leverage training available internally within the company and with universities and third-party training services. Monitor and grade each training provider and find replacements as necessary. Require all team members to attend foundational courses and recommend individuals attend specific trainings at the appropriate times given their job growth.

**Conduct periodic assessments of team members.**
Create a standardized record of each team member and update and review it periodically.

- Track how long the employee is in the current role, prior roles and tenure, education and training, and other pertinent information.
- Additionally, define key criteria to monitor given each team member's level in the organization and their growth goals. Criteria can include key competencies such as key knowledge areas and skills for the given role. Periodically measure the current level of the employee relative to the defined criteria and keep a record of past assessments to track how the employee has progressed over time. Identify any gaps and create a development plan (discussed next) to work on those areas.

**Create a development plan for each team member.**
Identify areas of development for each employee and work on a plan with the team member to develop those areas. Development areas can include items such as knowledge acquisition and the development of key skills. Consider the best way to develop each area including formal training, reading, coaching, and mentoring.

**Invest in team-building activities.**

Create regular opportunities for the team to connect informally and in a fun and relaxed way outside of the hustle and bustle of the day-to-day work. Team-building activities create team cohesion, improve morale, and allow team members to build relationships with one another. Organize activities that the specific team members find engaging and fun.

# 46

# PRODUCT MANAGER COMPETENCIES

*This reference section contains a list of important knowledge areas, abilities, and skills for product management.*

## Knowledge.

Knowledge includes topics, subject matter, and information that the Product Manager should know given their role and level in the organization. Knowledge is mental or theoretical rather than practical. Knowledge areas relevant to product management include:

- Expert-level knowledge of the product or product line
- Expert-level knowledge of the specific industry for the product or product line including target customers and competitors
- Ideation
- Innovation
- Business strategy
- Business models
- New product processes including Waterfall and Lean
- The Marketing Mix
- Product marketing
- Sales
- Finance
- Statistics

## Abilities and Skills.

An ability is being able to do something whereas a skill is being able to do that thing well. Abilities are usually innate, whereas skills are acquired through training.

Knowledge and abilities combine to create skills. Key Product Manager abilities and skills include the following:

- **Communication**
  - Active listening
  - Note-taking
  - Creating meeting minutes
  - Reporting status, verbal and written
  - Whiteboarding
  - Creating and giving presentations
  - Providing product training
  - Conducting product demos
- **Leadership and influence**
  - Building relationships, internally and externally
  - Gaining stakeholder buy-in for the product vision and strategy
  - Securing the needed resources for new product projects
  - Leading the product team through the inevitable challenges of developing a new product
  - Garnering support for trade-off decisions
  - Organizing and running meetings
  - Managing people
  - Negotiating, internally and with customers
- **Analysis**
  - Industry, market, and competitive analysis
  - Market research
  - Sizing a market
  - Revenue forecasting
  - Customer interviews and user testing
  - Experiment design and analysis
  - Evidence-based decision-making
  - Synthesizing large data sets and drawing actionable conclusions
  - Defining and tracking metrics
- **Planning and development**
  - Time-management
  - Setting an innovation strategy
  - Defining a business model

  - Building a Business Case
  - Articulating market needs and product requirements
  - Creating user personas
  - Prioritizing product features
  - Creating and managing the Product Roadmap
  - Rapid prototyping
  - Setting and managing a budget
  - Creating a risk management plan
  - Allocating resources
  - Conducting beta testing
  - Facilitating retrospectives
  - Retiring a product
- **Pricing**
  - Estimating value
  - Measuring willingness to pay
  - Pricing a new product
  - Pricing over the product life cycle
  - Reacting to competitive price changes
- **Marketing**
  - Segmenting a market
  - Positioning a product
  - Creating key product messages
  - Creating and executing a Launch Plan and a Marketing Plan
  - Creating Sales Enablement including product collateral and training
  - Providing media briefings and interviews
- **Technical**
  - Mastering the technical concepts and vocabulary specific to the industry and product
  - Software development including basic coding
  - User Experience (UX)
  - Spreadsheet and database software analysis tools
  - Presentation software

# 47

# PRODUCT MANAGER DELIVERABLES

*This reference section contains a list of common Product Manager deliverables throughout the product life cycle. The deliverables will vary depending on the scope of the role and the industry. Use the list when doing team workload planning, writing job descriptions, or considering how the capacity of the Product organization needs to evolve.*

## Discovery.

- Innovation Strategy for a product or product line
- Industry, Market, and Competitive Analysis
- Product SWOT Analysis
- Market Research

## Planning.

- Product Vision Statement
- Product Strategy
- Business Model Canvas
- Business Case
- Product Requirements
- Epics and User Stories
- Product Roadmaps
- Profit and Loss Statement
- Pricing Strategy and Pricing Policy
- Revenue Forecast

**Development, launch, marketing, end-of-life.**

- Beta Plan
- Segmentation, Targeting, and Positioning
- Messaging
- Launch Plan
- Input to the Marketing Plan
- Input to the Sales Enablement Plan and assist with deliverables
  - Customer qualification criteria
  - Product presentations
  - Datasheets
  - One-page product summary
  - Whitepapers
  - Sales scripts
  - Email templates
  - Customer success case studies
  - Competitor comparisons and competitor selling collateral
  - FAQ
- Product Training
- Product Demos
- Quarterly Business Review (QBR) Reports
- End-of-Life Plan

# 48

# ITEMS COMMON TO PRODUCT DOCUMENTS

*Several sections are often included in product documents and plans. This section summarizes the most common and is a convenient reference that you can review to determine if a given section should be included in a document or plan you or your team are creating.*

**Executive summary.**

An executive summary is useful if the document is more than three pages long. Although the summary is placed at the beginning of the document, it's best to write it last, summarizing the key aspects of the document. Invest time in creating a compelling summary as this may be the only section some readers read. The summary should contain the essence of the body of the document: the why, who, what, when, and where. Use hyperlinks to other sections of the document to allow the reader to quickly navigate to a section should they want to know more.

**Conclusions and recommendations.**

Don't leave it to the reader to draw their own conclusions. Instead, be explicit about the conclusions from the given analysis. Also, offer guidance and recommendations on how to proceed given those conclusions.

**Assumptions.**

Assumptions are things or events that are accepted as true or as certain to happen. Assumptions are often necessary during planning to allow a team to proceed. It's important to document key assumptions because, if they turn out to be false, it could have a materially negative impact on the outcome.

**Risks.**

Risks are uncertain events or conditions that, if they occur, will have a negative impact. Risks should be identified, quantified regarding the probability of occurrence and the potential impact, and mitigated against (see the risk management section).

**Issues.**

Issues are risks that have come to pass. Issues are usually items that are "open" and need to be resolved to get the project back on track.

**Dependencies.**

A dependency is when the output of one activity is needed for another activity. Product projects rarely operate in isolation, so it's important to document key tasks, activities, teams, customers, or other things upon which the success of the project is dependent.

**Revision history.**

A revision history is useful to track the date each version of the document was released, the changes in each version, and who made the changes. The version number should be visible on the first page of the document.

# 49

## TEAM MEETINGS

*Team meetings are useful to build team cohesion, as an efficient way to share and discuss items that have an impact at the team level, and to ensure alignment on key team activities. Key steps and best practices in organizing and running team meetings are discussed below.*

**Decide on the right cadence for team meetings.**

One of the key drawbacks of meetings, in general, is that they are costly, both in terms of time and money. Calculate the hourly cost of having the full team meet and use that to determine if a meeting is valuable or not. There is a limited number of productive hours a week for a team, and if they are overloaded with meetings, productivity will suffer. Decide if a meeting should be held repeatedly or as needed. Consider the costs and benefits of each. Sometimes a recurring meeting is required, especially if the team consists of members who are geographically dispersed.

**Manage the agenda.**

The team leader or manager should own and manage the meeting agenda. As part of the meeting planning process, seek input from the team on agenda items for the next meeting ahead of time. Keep a list of recurring agenda items to consider and note things that should be discussed in the next team meeting when you become aware of them throughout the work week. Common agenda items for Product Management team meetings include:

- Action items from the prior meeting
- Items related to new product projects
- Items related to customers (wins, losses, issues)

- Financial results review
- Competitor updates
- Review of recent market research
- Key decisions to make or that have been made
- Issues
- Updates from the Leadership Team
- Organization updates (changes, new hires, etc.)
- Upcoming planning work
- Upcoming team travel and time off
- Upcoming corporate events
- Team events and fun

**Cancel the meeting if it's not needed.**
Decide no later than two days before the meeting whether a meeting is warranted given the agenda and if the meeting is not needed, cancel it.

**Lead the team meeting.**
Always start and end on time. The manager should take meeting notes or assign someone to take the notes and send them to the manager afterward. Hold people accountable; if attendees are regularly showing up late or unprepared, have a private conversation with them to discuss the issue. Close the meeting with a summary of key action items resulting from the meeting.

**Distribute meeting minutes promptly.**
The team leader or manager should distribute meeting minutes noting attendees, key agenda items discussed, important notes, and action items within 24 hours of the meeting. Action items should have an owner and a due date.

# 50

## ONE-ON-ONE MEETINGS

*One-on-One (1:1) meetings are a great way for a manager to support the Product Managers on their team. There are many benefits of these informal meetings for both the manager and the Product Manager including allowing the manager to understand the status of key business objectives and stay aligned with the Product Manager, to discuss obstacles and how the manager can help, to get a sense of employee morale, as a coaching opportunity, and for both parties to share information on the organization and product projects.*

### Schedule recurring 1:1 meetings.

One-on-one meetings should occur every other week for 30 to 60 minutes. Meetings should be scheduled as recurring meetings, ideally at the same time each week the meeting occurs. If a meeting needs to be rescheduled, it should be rescheduled as close as possible to the original date to keep the overall 1:1 schedule on track.

### Consider the best location for the 1:1.

The ideal atmosphere for a 1:1 is informal, open yet private. Consider holding 1:1 meetings in a neutral location and not, for example, in the manager's office. That could include informal meeting rooms, the cafeteria, or going for a walk outside.

### Identify what to discuss.

It's best to avoid a formal agenda. Both the Product Manager and the manager should keep their own ongoing list of things to cover in the next 1:1 meeting and add to that list as things arise during the work day and work week. When the 1:1 meeting begins, both the manager and Product Manager should spend a couple of minutes creating a list of things both want to cover. Common items to discuss in 1:1 meetings include:

- Check-in on key business objectives and status
- Key impending deadlines and status
- Discussion of obstacles the Product Manager is facing, potential solutions, and identification of things the manager can do to help
- Workload
- Morale
- Team dynamics
- Personal development
- Feedback on the manager's working style
- General information sharing

# 51

# QUARTERLY BUSINESS REVIEW (QBR)

*An in-depth review of the business each quarter is a great way to ensure the product management team is on track to meet the key business objectives. Having each Product Manager present to the wider team on their area of business and product responsibility enables the team to strategize on challenges in each product area collectively and ensures that team members are aware of what's happening across different products. The QBR is also a good forcing function to have the Product Manager stop day-to-day work on the product and business area, step back, and consider how the product is performing relative to the overall product and business unit strategy.*

**Create and use a QBR template.**

Create a standardized template that will be used by each Product Manager in preparing for the QBR. Using a document is often better than using slides as it forces clarity of thought and prevents the Product Manager from spending time making the slides look good rather than thinking about the content of the report. Completing the template will take more effort the first time but each subsequent quarter it's likely that the Product Manager will be able to reuse and update some sections of the QBR report. Areas to cover in the QBR include:

- Market Update
  - Key market updates in the past quarter
  - Key market trends, their likely impact, and a recommended response
  - Key competitive changes in the past quarter
- Customer Update
  - Customer pipeline and engagement status

    - Customer wins and launches in the past quarter
    - Customer losses in the past quarter and a loss analysis
    - Customer engagements and meetings in the past quarter
    - Planned customer engagements for the next quarter
- Financial Update
    - Market size (TAM, SAM, and SOM) and a discussion on any changes in the past quarter
    - Review of past quarter's financial results
    - Review of the financial forecast and any material changes in the past quarter
    - Product profit and loss statement review and discussion on any changes
- Product Update
    - Releases in the past quarter
    - Review of active programs
    - Discussion of potential future products
    - Discussion on growing the business
- Dependencies
    - Status of key dependencies and discussion
- Business Objectives
    - Discussion of long-term goals
    - Status of current year goals
    - Accomplishments in the past quarter
    - Goals for the next quarter
- Risks, Issues, and Asks
    - Updates on prior risks and details of new risks and risk mitigation plans
    - Details of current issues and the plan to address those issues
    - Asks from the Product Manager to the management team

### Organize and run the QBR meeting.

The QBR meeting should be added to the team calendar a quarter or more in advance. If possible, have all team members attend the meeting in-person. Remind the team of the upcoming QBR meeting two weeks in advance and ask them to start working on their QBR report. Ask the individual Product Managers to complete and distribute the report at least three days before the meeting and ask each team member to review the other QBR reports ahead of the meeting and to come prepared with questions and feedback. Allow at least two hours per product during the QBR meeting and ask the presenting Product Manager to provide a summary of all areas from the QBR report and to discuss any areas in detail as they see fit. Don't cover more than two to three products per day as engagement will wane. Instead, spread the QBR over multiple days, if required, and cover only two to three products per day.

# 52

# PLANNING THE WORK WEEK AND DAY

*The team manager needs to be able to stay on top of their own workload and ensure that team members are likewise staying focused on the key business objectives. A methodical approach to project and task management will help the manager stay on track and not get overwhelmed. This section discusses one approach to managing the week's work, which draws on some of the concepts of the Getting Things Done® methodology from David Allen.*

## Keep all projects and tasks in one location.

Set up a database of all projects and tasks. This can be in paper form in a notebook, file system, digitally using Microsoft OneNote, Evernote, or any other project management software. The important thing is to capture all projects and tasks in one location. This takes effort to set up initially and discipline to maintain, but the payoff is tremendous. Sections of the notebook for a product management manager could include:

- All Projects
  - A list of all of the team's active projects. There are many times when it's convenient to be able to quickly review all active projects, for example, when having prioritization discussions or doing workload balancing.
- Goals
  - Long-term goals
  - Goals for this year
  - Goals for this quarter
- Key Projects
  - Sections for each key project. Projects can be grouped logically, for example, by market segment, product line, or product.

- Customers
    - Projects and tasks related to customer work; can be grouped as necessary.
- People
    - Create sections for key people with whom you interact including your manager, each team member, and key peers. This is particularly useful to assist with weekly one-on-one meetings.
    - Have a section with notes for future team meetings.
- Other
    - This can include things such as expenses, logistics, or any other areas where there is work to be done.

## Planning the work week.

Spend an hour each week doing a comprehensive review of all projects and tasks. The "weekly review" is the second critical discipline in order to stay organized and focused on the key business objectives. Conduct the review at the same time each week to build and maintain the habit. The review could be done at the end of the work week in preparation for the following week or first thing at the beginning of a given week. The purpose of the weekly review is to update the database with all new tasks, review and update existing projects and tasks, and identify what needs to get done in the week ahead. Resist the temptation to address any of the projects or tasks during the review. Instead, focus on updating the database and identifying the work for the week ahead. Create a checklist of steps to take during the weekly review (the "Weekly Review Checklist") and use that to guide the review each week. Key steps include the following:

- **Add new tasks.** The first key step is to add any new tasks to the database. Do a review of key task sources, identify any new tasks, and add them to the database. Common task sources could include:
    - Email, texts, and messaging apps
    - Calendars
    - Meeting notes
    - Roadmaps
    - Paper notebooks
    - Loose paper and documents
    - Physical "inboxes"
    - Team status reports

- **Update projects and tasks.** Next, review all existing projects and tasks in the database. Remove any items that are completed and update any projects or tasks that have changed.
- **Identify the work for the next week.** Finally, identify the work for the next week. Gather all tasks for the week ahead in a separate section called "This Week." Book time on the calendar to work on all key items.

## Planning the work day.

Create a checklist of tasks to do at the beginning of each day, the "Daily Checklist," and refer to that each day to plan the day ahead. Setting up the day should take only about 10 minutes. Keep the Daily Checklist dynamic; add new recurring items as they arise and remove old items that are no longer relevant. Below are some key steps that should appear on the Daily Checklist:

- Start planning by reviewing your calendar for the day. Note how much free time is available outside of appointments and meetings to get other work done. Use this to guide how much work to add to the "Today" task list.
- Quickly scan all sources of new tasks (see the list above) and determine if a particular task needs to be done today, this week, or later.
- Add any tasks for the current day to the "Today" task list. Update the "This Week" task list with any items that need to be addressed during the current week and defer all others to be considered and processed during the weekly review.
- Review the full "This Week" task list again and extract any tasks that need to be done today and add them to the "Today" task list.
- Identify the top one or two items that need to get done today and block the necessary time to get those done, ideally at the start of the day. It's a good idea to have a few daily time slots booked ahead that can be used to work on the top priorities for that day.

# ABOUT KEVIN BRENNAN

Kevin Brennan was born and raised in Ireland, where he completed his Bachelor of Engineering Electronic Engineering in 1999. He moved to San Francisco the same year and since then has worked in product management and product marketing roles at software and semiconductor companies, such as Dolby Laboratories and Cypress Semiconductor. Kevin has an MBA from Santa Clara University and a Certificate of Business Excellence (COBE) from the Haas School of Business at U.C. Berkeley. Kevin is a Product Development and Management Association (PDMA) New Product Development Professional and a Certified Product Manager, Certified Product Marketing Manager, and Certified Innovation Leader through the Association of International Product Marketing and Management (AIPMM).

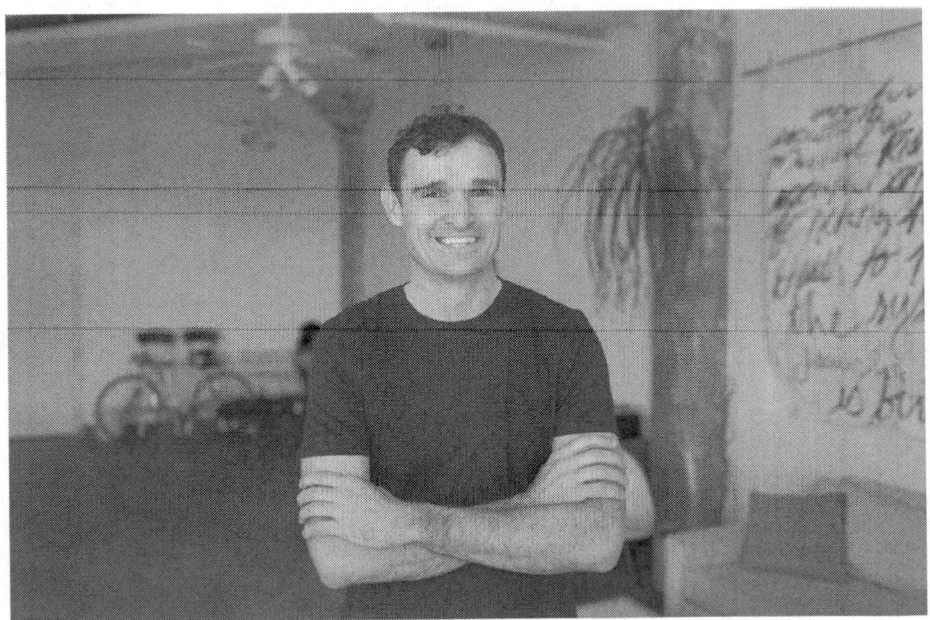

*If you enjoyed this book, please take a few moments to write a review of it. Thank you!*

Made in the USA
San Bernardino, CA
06 March 2020

65398040R00086